THE OLD BRITISH TONGUE

THE OLD BRITISH TONGUE

The Vernacular in Wales

1540 - 1640

by

R. BRINLEY JONES

Avalon Books

CARDIFF · 1970

Proprietors: Heanton Press Limited
Cardiff - 1970

SBN: 902294 00 8

To my revered and beloved father

JOHN ELIAS JONES

who died on the 14th April 1969
I dedicate this book as a token
of my gratitude always

*'Daioni a thrugaredd a'm canlynant holl
ddyddiau fy mywyd a phreswyliaf yn
nhŷ'r Arglwydd yn dragywydd.'*

PREFACE

This essay, in its original form, was conceived as an introduction to a semantic analysis of the Welsh vocabulary in the second half of the sixteenth century. Here it has been enlarged to include aspects of the vernacular movements in Italy, France and England which seem to be relevant to the study of the vernacular in Wales; this section, which forms the Introduction, is clearly indebted to the works of Richard Foster Jones, Vernon Hall and De Witt Starnes.

My interest in the period owes much to the distinguished scholarship of two of my former teachers, the late Professor G. J. Williams of Cardiff and Professor I. Ll. Foster of Oxford. I shall never be able to measure the debt I owe to both of them. The imperfections which remain in this work are, of course, my own responsibility.

I should like to record my gratitude to the directors of Avalon Books for their kindness in inviting me to contribute the first in their series of educational monographs, and to the printers who have taken so much care in the production of this book.

R.B.J.

University of Wales

CONTENTS

INTRODUCTION

IN THE realm of thought, the countries of Western Europe borrowed much from each other during the sixteenth century, and in terms of literary criticism and in the discussions evaluating the relative merits of the vernacular, France followed Italy and England followed France. Since the time of her medieval literary contacts, Wales never enjoyed such close relations with Western Europe as she did during the sixteenth century. The Middle Ages had largely been characterized by a uniformity in life and letters in which Wales had shared, and even if the political and religious revolutions of the sixteenth century in one sense hampered the means of renewing such contact, in another sense they strengthened it. The political changes made London an attractive centre for aspiring Welshmen, and together with the spirit that was sweeping across Europe, created a new influx into the universities. The religious changes sent refugees, Protestant and Catholic, to seek asylum in the cultural centres of the continent.

It was at Oxford, Cambridge and the Inns of Court in London that Welshmen most came into contact with men who had been moved to restore the dignity of their own vernacular. This contact proved as significant as the learning they found there. In 1574, Thomas Wiliems wrote of William Salesbury,

> W.S. meddaf yw Brutanaid dyscedicaf nid yn vnic yn y Vrutanaec, eithyr yn Ebrew, Groec, llatin, Sasonaec, Ffrancaec, Ellmynaec, ac eraill ieithiae, val y bai ryvedd gallu o vn gwr gyrheudd cyfryw perfeithrwyd yn y tavodae, oni bai nad ystudiai ddim arall tra vai vyw.[1]

But Oxford had done more than kindle in him an interest in languages; there he had met men who were devising ways of prospering their mother tongue. After leaving the university, Humphrey Lhuyd joined the Earl of Arundel's service as family physician; he thus came into immediate contact with one of the foremost Renaissance spirits in England.[2] Other young Welshmen served as retainers in such noble households as those of the earls of Pembroke, Leicester and Buckhurst, and here again they came into touch with the New Learning. In 1594 George Owen of Henllys refers to the numbers of Welshmen 'brought up and maintained at the universities of Oxford and Cambridge . . where some proved to be learned men and good members in the Commonwealth of England and Wales; some worthy labourers in the Lord's vineyard'.[3] Of such, John Prys, Richard Davies, Gruffydd Robert, Thomas Huet, Morys Clynnog, Siôn Dafydd Rhys, Henry Salesbury, Henri Perri, Huw Lewys, Edward James, Richard Parry, John Davies and Thomas Wiliems studied at Oxford and others such as William Morgan, Edmwnd Prys and Robert Holland studied at Cambridge.

Some found inspiration and guidance from intimate contact with continental scholars. Richard Davies was at Frankfurt from 1555 to 1558 where Richard Cox was one of the leading Protestant lights.[4] Gruffydd Robert not only travelled on the continent, but also became one of the distinguished company of Cardinal Borromeo's court. There, in Milan, was a real humanist coterie, with the Cardinal, himself widely travelled in Spain, France and Flanders, as its illustrious head.[5] Siôn Dafydd Rhys had been to Venice, Crete and Cyprus. He graduated in Medicine at Siena and taught at Pistoia; in 1569 he published DE ITALICA PRONUNCIATIONE at Padua.[6] Morris Kyffin had served as Surveyor of the Muster Rolls in the English army in the Low Countries, and in 1591 was with the forces in Normandy.[7]

Thus, in a real sense, young Welshmen, sons of the gentry and clergy of Wales, had come into contact with the prevailing modes in Italy, France and England in the sixteenth century. Stimulated as they were by the energies of the devotees of other vernaculars, and inspired by the work of translation they found in other languages, it is not surprising that they turned to Wales to show their own enthusiasm for their native tongue. They were too closely associated with the native literary tradition to apply without modification the methods which they discerned to be most valuable in other countries. Their particular service to Wales was that they were able to impose many of the current ideas of Western Europe on to the peculiar traditions of their own country.

So intimate was this contact with Western Europe that it is impossible to view the subject of the vernacular in Wales in isolation; it can only be understood as part of the wider canvas of the vernacular movements in England, France and Italy. It will be well to examine briefly the vicissitudes of such movements in order to estimate how much Wales was influenced by them and to see in which ways she modified many of their ideas to suit the mould of her own particular problems and conditions.

Italy

The 'questione della lingua' in Italy began with Dante, who defended the vernacular in the CONVIVIO and whose DE VULGARI ELOQUENTIA antedated remarks found in the later Renaissance prefaces. 'The literary triumph of the vernaculars is forecast in Dante', says C. S. Baldwin[8], but the fight was long and one of many vicissitudes. It was the DE VULGARI ELOQUENTIA however which influenced the work of later writers. The revived study of Latin by the humanists brought to light the deficiencies of the vernacular which for two centuries had gained some literary achievement. The real debate between the relative merits of Latin and Italian emerged when Italian itself was regaining literary eminence and when the desire of 'umanesimo volgare' was manifesting itself. In Italy, Latin was regarded by many as the supreme national language of the country, and so the sharp conflict which emerged in France and England did not as such appear in Italy.

There were conservative scholars who regarded the preserve of learning as the sole heritage of those conversant with Latin; such scholars remonstrated against the use of the vernacular in serious thought. But the strength of those who favoured the vernacular lay in the work of Dante, Petrarch and Boccaccio, which was proof enough of the intrinsic merit of the Italian language. As G. D. Willcock and A. Walker have remarked, 'In Italy the contest was fought out first, but the position of Italy was unique; a line of great Tuscan poets stretching back to Dante . . In Spain, Portugal, France, England, and to a certain extent in Germany . . Scholars assume or maintain that the vernaculars are bare and inadequate, not only limited by frontiers but incapable of carrying the heaviest guns'.[9] Wales, however, far more nearly presents a parallel with Italy. It, too, had a compelling literary past. It was this possibility of retrospection in Italy and Wales which became the strength, and indeed in large part, the solution, of the 'questione' in both these countries.

In the fifteenth century, Leon Battista Alberti, himself a humanist and author of many Latin works, believed that those unacquainted with Latin had a right to the benefits of learning. The vernacular was essential for the people at large; Italian was potentially rich, and only needed cultivation by learned men,

> Et chi sarà quello temerario che pure mi perseguiti, biasimando che io scriva in modo che l'uomo m'intenda? Piuttosto forse i prudenti mi loderanno, se io scrivendo in modo che lui non m'intenda, prima cerco giovare a molti, che piacere a pochi; . . Ben confesso quell' antica latina lingua essere copiosa molto, e ornatissima; ma non però veggo in che sia la nostra oggi toscana tanto da averla in odio, che in essa qualunque benchè ottima cosa scritta ci dispiaccia. . . E' sia quanto dicono, quella antica appresso di tutte le genti piena di autorità, solo perchè in essa molti dotti scrissero, simile certo sarà la nostra, s'e dotti la vorranno molto con suo studio e vigilie essere elimata e pulita[10] . .

It was such a sentiment of 'io scrivendo in modo che lui non m'intenda, prima cerco giovare a molti, che piacere a pochi' which became an important factor later in the vernacular movement in Wales, and prompted Morris Kyffin to translate the APOLOGIA into Welsh, though

> Duw a wyr e fuasse howsach i mi o lawer, a hynodach i'm henw, scrifenny'r cyfryw beth mewn iaith arall chwaethach nog yn Gymraec.[11]

Roger Ascham in the Dedication of TOXOPHILUS 1545, admitted that 'to have written this boke in latin or Greke . . had bene more easier'.[12] As Alberti said of Italian, so Gruffydd Robert claimed of Welsh, that though neglected, it was

> mor ḷaụnḷythr im scrifēnu, cyn gyfoethocced o eiriaụ, cyn hyned fynechreuad a'r falchaf o'r ieithocḍ a hēuais.[13]

It needed only cultivation to compare with other languages.

In his REGOLE GRAMMATICALI DELLA VOLGAR LINGUA of 1516, Francesco Fortunio illustrated how Italian, like Latin, was governed by grammatical precepts. In 1525 Pietro Bembo presented the claims and capacities of the vernacular and asserted that it was more capable of treating modern subjects than the ancient tongues were; his PROSE DELLA VOLGAR LINGUA was the manifesto of the 'questione' in Italy.

One of the primary aims of humanists in Italy as elsewhere was to bring learning to the court of the prince and to teach him and his retinue graceful and proper speech. Castiglione elaborated upon this in his IL CORTEGIANO, 1528, and it was something for which Gruffydd Robert showed concern in his title-page,

> DOSPARTH BYRR AR Y rhann gyntaf i ramadeg cymraeg ḷe cair ḷauer o bynciau anhepcor i vn a chụennychai na doedyd y gymraeg yn ḍilediaith, nai scrifennu'n iaụn.[14]

It was his contribution to a 'lingua cortigiana' in Wales. It was such an interest in correct speech among the upper classes too, which prompted Meigret in his RÉPONSE À L'APOLOGIE DE PELETIER, 1550, to address the courtiers of France as

> messieurs les courtizans e tous aotres qui font leur profession de bien parler,[15]

Indeed, the use of the vernacular by men of high degree was of some significance in the vernacular movement; in Italy, Gelli believed that the use of Italian by 'i principi e gli uomini grandi e qualificati' to express 'le importantissime cose' was of consequence.[16] As will be seen, similar sentiments were expressed in Wales.

Owing to the association between prince and language in Italy (and later in France), there were those who advocated the speech of the court as the ideal. This was elaborated by Vincenzo Colli in his POESIA VOLGARE, by Mario Equicola in DELLA NATURA DI AMORE, and by Baldassare Castiglione in IL CORTEGIANO. It was partly as a reaction against this courtly usage that the 'questione' came to a head in the sixteenth century. There were those who advocated Tuscan as the literary standard, among them two groups, one represented by Pietro Bembo and Salviati who viewed Tuscan of the fourteenth century as the ideal (this eventually received more or less general acceptance); the other, represented by Machiavelli, Tolomei, Gelli, Giambullari and Varchi, who wished to adopt Tuscan of the day, though they differed among themselves as to the standard to be adopted. There were the anti-Tuscan spirits, too, who favoured a composite language comprising elements common to all the Italian dialects. This group found a precedent in Dante who described his ideal in DE VULGARI ELOQUENTIA as an

> illustre, cardinale, aulicum et curiale vulgare in Latio, quod

> omnis latiae civitatis est et nullius esse videtur.[17]

Much of the history of the vernacular movement in Italy is concerned with the debate over dialect. William Salesbury, writing primarily in the North Welsh dialect claimed, 'Neq equū sit me subiici Demetarū iudicio, . . '[18] and although John Davies adjudged *ws* as 'vulgo demetarum'[19] and *iff* 'quae nunquam sine indignatione audio',[20] the difference never assumed either importance or difficulty for any writer in Wales.

Rhetoric was, at this time, once again very much the 'ars bene dicendi',[21] and as Henri Perri affirmed, it was used to quicken all languages,

> Nid vn iaith sy'n gnotay, ac yn benthyccio echwynborth gan honn: anid pob iaith . . sy'n eiriol arni am adhbhwyndeb, rhac trwscl annhrebhn, ac ammorth.[22]

Gelli believed that the orators would do much to augment the vernacular in Italy,

> . . che e' sono solamente gli uomini grandi e virtuosi quelli che inalzano e fanno grandi le lingue; imperrochè, avendo sempre concetti nobili e alti, a trattando e maneggiando cose di gran momento, e ragionando bene spesso e discorrendo sopra quelle in pro e in contro, persuadendo o dissuadendo, accusando o lodando, e talvolta ancora ammonendo e insegnando, fanno le lingue loro copiose, onorate, ricche e leggiadre.[23]

By the end of the sixteenth century, the Italian language was foremost in literary and humanistic works. This was the result not only of the vigorous defence of the vernacular, but of the conscious polishing and codification of it, achieved by the labours of men like Fortunio and Bembo. In 1582 the Florentine Academy was succeeded by the Academia della Crusca which published a dictionary of the Italian language in 1612.

France

At the end of the fifteenth century, Latin was still the language of learning in France, but the sixteenth century witnessed a culmination of forces which brought about the final emergence of the vernacular.[24] National pride, universal curiosity and the discovery and utilization of the art of printing were factors of vital importance in bringing the issue to a head. Also many

French students began to attend the Italian universities and the success of the vernacular there gave a firm impetus to the cause of the French language in much the same way as was to happen later to the young Welsh humanists during their stay at the universities. Many of the theories of the 'questione' in Italy were borrowed and modified by scholars like du Bellay in France.

By the beginning of the sixteenth century, French society was emerging out of its feudal character and embarking upon its history of absolute monarchy, and with it came the desire for unification. The monarchs of France realised the unifying force of the vernacular, and with the *Ordonnances de Villers-Cotterêts* of 1539 came the official pronouncement favouring the vernacular. It sanctioned the use of French in public and private contracts and in the courts of justice. It was the very antithesis of the 1536 Act of Union in Wales.

Absolutism brought with it national pride, which though minimized by Professor R. Foster Jones as a contribution to the cause of the vernacular in England,[25] was of major importance in France. The activities of the *Pléiade*, a group of writers to which Joachim du Bellay belonged and among which Pierre de Ronsard was chief, were motivated by this patriotism. Du Bellay wrote,

> la mesme loy naturelle, qui commande à chacun défendre le lieu de sa naissance, nous oblige aussi de garder la dignité de notre langue[26]

and Ronsard speaks

> et prendre pitié, comme bons enfans, de leur pauvre mère naturelle[27]

It was the sentiment expressed by Gruffydd Robert,

> rhaid ymy ḍamuno ar bob cymro bonheḍig, a rhoụiog, na bo mụy annaturiol i mi, nog yụ pobl erail̦ i iaith i mammau[28]

As has been implied, French was still regarded as being inferior to Latin at the beginning of the sixteenth century, but the attempt to cultivate Ciceronian Latin proved abortive and paved the way for the success of the vernacular. There was abroad a certain democratic spirit which demanded that the vistas of the new learning be made available to all. The first public champion of French, Geoffroy Tory, set out to convince the learned that

> avec les gens de bonnes lettres le peuple commun puisse

> user des livres.[29]

French was the language of 'le peuple commun'.

Of great significance in the social structure of sixteenth-century France was the evolution of the middle class, and in its shadow came Protestantism and the vernacular. In 1523 there appeared a translation of the New Testament by Lefèvre d'Étaples, designed that

> les simples membres du corps de Jésus-Christ, ayant ce en leur langue, puissent estre aussi certains de la vérité évangélique comme ceulx qui l'ont en latin.[30]

In his preface the translator addressed

> docteurs de la loy, qui avez osté la clef de science; vous n'y estes point entrez et avez empesché ceulx qui y entroyent . . Et comment prescheront-ilz à garder toute chose que Jésus-Christ a commandé: se ilz ne veulent point que le simple peuple voye et lise en sa langue l'évangile de Dieu?[31]

It met with some opposition and the Sorbonne forbade translations, asserting that apart from the impossibility of rendering Latin scriptural terms, French was itself completely insufficient. As Rotier put it in DE NON VERTENDA SCRIPTURA SACRA IN VULGAREM LINGUAM,

> Lingua enim vernacula et popularis ieiuna est et inops.[32]

But the issue was decided outside the university. With the swift translation from its Latin form, the INSTITUTION DE LA RELIGION CHRÉTIENNE of John Calvin in 1540 started a whole stream of polemical literature, both Protestant and Catholic, in the vernacular, from which French emerged as the language of theological debate.

The first concern of the scholars of the sixteenth century was defence of the vernacular, and early in the century, writers upheld its latent potentialities. Geoffroy Tory claimed that France had been a centre of learning before the Romans came, and that it was with the invasion by Caesar that the true culture of France had been lost. This belief enhanced in his mind the prestige of the language whose superiority he declared in 1529,

> Notre langue est une des plus belles et gracieuses de toutes les langues humaines[33]

– a sentiment which was reiterated by Henri Estienne in his LA

PRÉCELLENCE DU LANGAGE FRANÇOIS of 1579:

nostre langue Françoise surmonte toutes les vulgaires.[34]

Soon the same scholars became concerned with the problem of embellishment. But among them there was not entire conformity of opinion as to how this might be achieved. Some favoured foreign importations; the patriotism of others frowned upon such un-French elements. Apart from conscious neologizing, French had gained new words from Spanish and a few German words brought by the German-Swiss mercenary troops. But the greatest foreign element was Italian, and though such words as *burlesque*, *assassin*, *banque*, *façade*, and *cabinet* reveal how acceptable such terms became, there was opposition to the Italian importations. Ronsard, du Bellay and Henri Estienne opposed the numerous borrowed terms of war and amusement brought in by the court. Henri Estienne was particularly opposed to them. Ronsard, preferring the exploitation of the native elements of the vernacular commended the creation of one part of speech from another. Both Peletier and Ronsard favoured the reintroduction of what, in England, Sir John Cheke called 'the old denisoned wordes',[35]

Respectez la langue française, ne battez pas votre mère. Je vous recommande par testament les vieux mots français que l'on veut remplacer par des termes empruntés du latin . .[36]

and though the movement in France never attempted to recall the literary past to the extent that it was recalled in Italy and Wales, Ronsard remarked,

Encore vaudroit il mieux comme un bon Bourgeois ou Citoyen, rechercher et faire un Lexicon des vieils mots d'Artus, Lancelot et Gauvain, on commenter le Romant de la Rose, que s'amuser à je ne sçay quelle Grammaire latine qui a passé son temps.[37]

It is interesting to remember how in Wales Sir Thomas Wiliems explained why some people found difficulty in understanding William Salesbury's translation of the New Testament,

A chyd bair andyscedic yn beiaw ar ei ymchweliad ir Camberaec (o bleit buan y barn pob ehud) eto y neb a ddarlleno Cronic y Brutanieid ar tywysogion, Cyfrai(th) hoell dda ap Cadell, cywyddae a cherddae prydyddion celfydd yn yr iaith y Cyfraith Camberaec a welawdd ef, ac amryw o hen lyvrae, Siarterae ac eraill o hen goffae . . [38]

Dialect too, was to be used to augment the resources of the tongue; the early supremacy of Francien prevented the battle of dialect which assumed such importance in Italy. Ronsard in his ABREGE DE L'ART POETIQUE FRANÇOIS 1565 commended the introduction of dialect words on the pretext that classical languages had themselves been enriched in that way. But his commendation held a rider,

> Je te conseilles d'user indifféremment de tous dialectes, comme j'ay desja dit, entre lesquels le courtisan est tousjours le plus beau, à cause de la majesté du prince.[39]

Joachim du Bellay's DEFENSE ET ILLUSTRATION DE LA LANGUE FRANÇOISE, 1549, was the manifesto of the vernacular movement in France. Dr. Bernard Weinberg has summarised the intention of the work, 'to defend French against its detractors and against those who prefer Greek and Latin to it, and to indicate ways in which French may be raised to the level of excellence of the classical languages.'[40] Du Bellay deplored the disparagement of the language and emphasized the need for its cultivation and for its being used by men of 'grand-érudition', men of 'uchelddysc' as the Welsh would have said, the means by which Italian had gained esteem. His precepts resolved themselves into two – the creation of new words and the reintroduction of old. Borrowings were to be made with modesty:

> Je voudroy' bien que nostre langue feust si riche d'exemples domestiques, que n'eussions besoing d'avoir recours aux étrangers.[41]

In a letter written by him to Jean de Morel, he referred to the value of compound words and cited some of his own coinings, *pié-sonnant*, *porte-ciel* and *porte-lois*.

The rôle of the printer and publisher in the vernacular movement is of great significance; not only was he in control of this great new means of dissemination, but often he seemed imbued with a missionary spirit in the cause of the vernacular. Caxton had been an earnest supporter in England;[42] Wales too, had its servants – Thomas Salisbury, 'a bookbinder dwelling in Powles Churchyard'[43] first used his imprint on Henry Salesbury's GRAM-

MATICA BRITANNICA 1593. In France, two of the greatest champions of the vernacular were printers, Geoffroy Tory and Robert Estienne.

There were those scholars who realized that the future of the vernacular depended on its acquiring some of the stability and regularity which distinguished Latin. Printing emphasized the need for such fixity. Robert Estienne published a small volume on the conjugation of French verbs in 1530, and composed a Latin dictionary in 1531, accompanied by a translation of Latin words into French, which was reprinted with a number of additions in 1536. In 1538 he published his DICTIONARIUM LATINO-GALLICUM, and 1539-40 his DICTIONNAIRE FRANÇOIS-LATIN; several concise school editions of both were re-issued frequently.

As in Italy, so in France, there was a desire to establish a 'bel usage', and the French writers too turned to the language of the court as the ideal. Meigret, the great exponent of courtly speech in France, said of words which were not used by the courtier, 'Il ne faut donc l'employer'.[44] Gradually the canon of usage became the consent of a learned academy. The official concern for the language – its stability and standard – was passed to the French Academy when Richelieu gave that body his blessing in 1635.

England

In England too, the Renaissance spirit brought with it a curiosity and a demand to participate in all the fields of learning which had hitherto been regarded as the preserve of the few, but the demand was not without some disapprobation.[45] Sir Thomas Hoby's epistle, dated 1556, prefixed to his translation of IL CORTEGIANO alluded to the fact that

> our learned menne for the moste part hold opinion, to haue the sciences in the mother tunge, hurteth memorie and hindreth lerning.[46]

However, such academic objections proved unavailing; Sir Thomas Wilson made reference to the thirst for knowledge which the new spirit had created in the minds of men:

> For, considering the forwardenesse of this age, wherein the very multitude are prompte & ripe in al Sciences that haue by any mans diligence bene sett forth vnto them: . . And

> farther pōdering that diuerse learned mē of other coūtreis have heretofore for the furtheraunce of knowlege, not suffred any of the Sciences liberal to be hidden in the Greke, or Latine tongue, but have with most earnest trauaile made every of them familiar to their vulgare people: I thought that Logique . . myght with as good grace be sette forth in Thenglishe . .[47]

A character in a work by William Stafford in 1581 inquired whether it might be possible to have the works of Vigetius and Columella

> in our English tongue, and read them ouer though we neuer wente to schoole.[48]

There was among the educated a feeling of social responsibility to share with others the benefits of knowledge. Fabian Wither condemned those who

> as though they were borne only for themselves and to their own uses, haue altogether neglected to publish or set forth any thing for the common commoditie of their countrey.[49]

in much the same spirit as Thomas Wiliems later regarded the sharing of his dictionary,

> . . nys galhwn ag ny dhylywn gadw'n briotol ymyhun y peth a dhylei vod yn gyphredin y laweroedh o herwydh y mowrles a'r budhiant, . . a dhaw ag a dyf o honaw.[50]

Ironically, the Latin tradition suffered as a result of the excessive ardour of the humanists, who, in their efforts to restore Latin on the pattern of the style and vocabulary of Cicero, contributed to the cause of the vernacular. As Ascham put it in TOXOPHILUS in 1545

> as for the Latin or greke tonge, euery thyng is so excellently done in them, that none can do better.[51]

The dissemination of knowledge was made possible practically by the art of printing, the invention of which was regarded in retrospect by Silvester Jourdan in 1610

> the admirable art of Printing . . an inuention so excellent and so vsefull, so much tending to the honour of God, the manifestation of the truth, propagation of the Gospell, restoration of learning, diffusion of knowledge . .[52]

Paper had become cheaper and it was to the commercial advantage of the printer to publish books in the mother tongue, the market for which would naturally be much greater than for the classics. The position is recapitulated in a remark made by an Elizabethan printer to Thomas Drant in 1567,

> Though, sir, your book be wise and full of learning, yet peradventure it will not be so saleable.[53]

For many, printing was regarded as a providential discovery – and that understood literally. In 1547 John Prys had said

> Ac yr awr y rhoes duw y prynt yn mysk ni er amylhau gwybodaeth y eireu bendigedic ef,[54]

Reference is made in Foxe's ACTS AND MONUMENTS of 1632 to

> that inestimable benefit of Gods blessing, prepared for the behoofe of his Church, I meane the singuler and most excellent Art of Emprinting.[55]

The Reformation in religion removed authority from the Church to the Bible, and consequently, translation of Holy Scripture became an integral part of Protestantism. After the translation of Scripture there emanated a whole stream of controversial literature, and it was in the interest of the Romans to reply to the attacks and claims in the language of the people. There was a pretext for religion in the vernacular; the seed had been sown. From the time that Wycliffe had employed English, one of the strongholds of Latin had been impaired. With the Reformation came a desire to instruct the people, and Hugh Goughe explained in 1570

> I haue translated into our vulgar speche, this little booke, that herein, the vnacquainted with the latine tounge, may learne reade and see the sume of their belefe.[56]

Centralized monarchy, the changed political and social conditions, and the break with Rome culminated to effect a new feeling of independence in England. Nicholas Grimald was cognizant of the diffusion of classical knowledge which was taking place in other countries of Western Europe. His purpose in translating Cicero was

> to do likewise for my countriemen: as Italians, Frenchmen, Spaniardes, Dutchmen, and other foreins haue liberally done for theyrs.[57]

This same patriotic determination impelled Henry Billingsley in 1570 to affirm

> our Englishe tounge shall no lesse be enriched with good Authors, then are other straunge tounges: as the Dutch, French, Italian, and Spanishe: in which are red all good authors in a maner, founde amongest the Grekes or Latines.[58]

And the cause of the vernacular in England, as in other countries, found further encouragement in the realization that Latin and Greek had been vernaculars in their day. The translator of Peter Ramus' LOGIKE posed the question thus

> . . Did Cicero who was a Latinist borne write his Philosophie and Rethorike in the Greke tongue? or was he content with his mother tongue?[59]

Though there were many who supported the cause of the vernacular, few of them were unwilling to concede to its inadequacy as a medium of expression for the expanding content of sixteenth century thought. Ralph Lever epitomised the dilemma in 1573

> I see and confesse, that there be Plura rerum, quam verborum genera, (that is, moe things, then there are words to expresse things by)[60]

This difficulty was encountered by Caxton in 1481. He spoke of translating a Dutch tale 'in to this rude and symple englyssh'.[61] The Bishop of Durham in 1499 compared the insufficiency of English with the 'perfeccyon' of Latin.[62] But classical standards were not the only ones which made poignant the deficiencies of the vernacular. It suffered even in comparison with modern languages

> Yet betwene frenche and englysshe is grete deffens.
> Their longage In redynge is douse and dylycate.
> In theyr mother tonge they be so fortunate.
> They haue the bybyll and the apocalypys of devynyte,
> With other nobyll bokes that in Englyche may not be.[63]

This feeling of despondency which characterized writers' remarks was not occasioned by ignorance of the native tradition; there were those who looked back with gratitude to the writers of the fourteenth century. Pynson in 1526 expressed how Chaucer

> by his labour
> embelyshed
> ornated

and made fayre our englysshe[64]

and John Rastell spoke highly of Gower, Chaucer and Lydgate

By these men our tong is amplyfyed so
That we therin now translate as well may
As in eny other tongis other can do . .[65]

Nevertheless, despite Sherry's tribute to

> the most excellent monumentes of our aũciẽt forewriters, Gower, Chawcer and Lydgate[66]

their influence on the wider field of language in the sixteenth century was circumscribed. The impact of their work is found primarily in the poetry of Skelton, Hawes, Wyatt, Surrey and Grimald, and did not become as did fourteenth century literature in Wales and Italy, a source of general inspiration in the vernacular movement or a fund of so much verbal deposit for utilization in prose. As Gladys Willcock and Alice Walker have said in their introduction to Puttenham's THE ARTE OF ENGLISH POESIE: 'It is very noticeable how, particularly in the pamphlets of Du Bellay and Sidney, it is faith in the latent capacities of the language and in the native genius, rather than respect for past literary achievements, which provides the rock of their defence'.[67]

Because Latin had held the monopoly of scholarship during the Middle Ages, English remained undeveloped along certain avenues of thought, and translation from the classics, an essential element of humanist literary activity, immediately revealed the 'lacunae' of the English vocabulary. Gawin Douglas in his preface to the translation of the AENEID in 1553 quoted Latin words which he found difficult to convey;[68] and a writer of 1530 stated

> Yt is not lyght for euery man to drawe eny longe thyng from latyn in to oure Englyshe tongue. For there ys many wordes in Latyn that we haue no propre englyssh accordynge therto.[69]

Among works which patently illustrated the inadequacy of the vernacular were those which treated the technicalities of art and science. Robert Recorde observed in 1547

> considering that it is more harder to translate into such a tonge, wherein the arte hath not ben written before, then to write in those tongues that are accustomed, and (as I might say) acquainted with the terms of the science.[70]

William Rastell encountered the same difficulty in 1557 in the niceties of the legal vocabulary. Referring to the statutes, he remarked

> For those that were first written in latin or in frenche, dare I not presume to translate into Englishe, for feare of misse interpretacion. For many wordes and termes be there in diuers statutes, both in latyn and in frenche, which bee very hard to translate aptly into English.[71]

And even when English had gained ground and prestige there were those serious scholars, Bacon among them, who questioned its durability.

There were enthusiastic defenders of English in the sixteenth century, among them Elyot, Ascham, Wilson, Puttenham and Mulcaster. Partly as a result of their labours, and partly as a result of the 'many excellent writers' of the day as Holinshed observed in 1577, the attitude to the vernacular changed. Mr. F. W. Bateson suggests 'The turning-point is in or about 1590. At this period a new respect for the English language, rising in some cases to a perfervid enthusiasm, begins to make itself heard'.[72] Professor R. Foster Jones would relate this change to the years 1575–1580,[73] though Veré L. Rubel suggests that 'By 1557 it was generally held that English had become adequate, even abundant'.[74] William Salesbury remarked in 1547 that he had compiled his DICTIONARY

> . . ir hai hynny yn vnic o chwenychant vegys y dylent hynny kyfrwyddyt i ddarllen a deall iaith Saesnec iaith heddyw vrddedic o bob rhyw oreuddysc iaith gyflawn o ddawn a buddygoliaeth . .[75]

Andrew Borde reflected on the change in 1548

> The speche of Englande is a base speche to other noble speches, as Italion, Castylion, and Frenche; howbeit the speche of Englande of late dayes is amended.[76]

In 1593 Harvey said that English was

> never so furnished or embellished as of late[77]

and Robert Parry in the preface to MODERATUS, OR THE ADVENTURES OF THE BLACK KNIGHT, 1595

> . . which language is growne nowe to be so copious, that it may compare with most of the richest tongues in all *Europe*, such is the carefull industrie of our Countrimen . . to amplifie the same.[78]

In 1598 Florio spoke of

> the copie and varietie of our sweete-mother-toong, which under this most Excellent Princesse is growne farre beyond that of former times.[79]

Miss Gladys Willcock has commented that 'By the end of the century the *défense et illustration* were complete'[80] and indicative of that change was Richard Carew's EPISTLE ON THE EXCELLENCY OF THE ENGLISH TONGUE, 1595–1596 inspired by Henri Estienne's PROJET DU LIVRE INTITULÉ DE LA PRÉCELLENCE DU LANGAGE FRANCOIS.

Writers thought the vernacular worthy of comparison with other languages. Sherry remarked in 1550

> Good cause haue we therefore to gyue thankes unto certayne godlye and well learned men, whych by their greate studye enrychynge our tongue both wyth matter and wordes, haue endeuoured to make it so copyous and plentyfull that therein it maye compare wyth anye other whiche so euer is the best.[81]

Richard Eden was more specific in a letter which he wrote to Sir William Cecil in 1562

> the Latine toonge be accompted ryche, and the Englysshe indigent and barbarous, as it hathe byn in tyme past, muche more then it nowe is, before it was enriched and amplyfied by sundry bookes in manner of all artes translated owt of Latine and other toonges into Englysshe . .[82]

Ralph Holinshed claimed in 1577 that

> there is no one speache vnder the sonne spoken in our time, that hath or can haue more varietie of words, copie of phrases, or figures or floures of eloquence, then hath our Englishe tongue . .[83]

The methods by which Englishmen achieved adequacy of vocabulary in the sixteenth century were partly described by Ralph Lever in 1573

> Yet is there this help in speach, that we ofte vse manye wordes to expresse one thing: yea and sometimes one word is vsed to signifie sundry matters. Moreouer, one language borroweth from another, and where there is want, men sometimes deuise newe names and compounded termes.[84]

The process of translation from the classics not only convinced the writer of the inadequacy of English but encouraged him to assimilate into the vocabulary words which were difficult to translate. At the same time, intellectual and other commerce with France, Italy and Spain brought with it words from those vernaculars. In 1571 Thomas Digges justified his borrowing from the classical languages

> . . let no man muse that writing in the English toung, I haue retained the Latin or Greeke names of sundry lines and figures, as cordes Pentagonall, lines Diagonall, . . for as the Romanes and other Latin writers . . haue not shamed to borrow of the Grecians these and many other terms of arte: so surely do I thinke it no reproche, either to the English tongue, or any English writer, where fit words faile to borowe of them both . .[85]

George Pettie in 1581 defended his neologising on the pretext that other modern vernaculars and classical languages employed the same means of embellishment:

> And though for my part I vse those words as litle as any, yet I know no reason why I should not vse them, and I finde it a fault in my selfe that I do not vse them: for it is in deed the ready way to inrich our tongue, and make it copious, and it is the way which all tongues haue taken to inrich them selues:[86]

Mulcaster described the extent of this language commerce in 1582; English, he said,

> boroweth dailie from foren tungs, either of pure necessitie in new matters, or of mere brauerie, to garnish it self with all . . The necessitie of these foren words must nedes be verie great bycause the number of them is so verie manie.[87]

Many of these new-coined terms would need explanation. Some writers maintained that frequent usage would make current their meanings

> . . long vse hath made these woords curraunt: and why may not vse doo as much for these woords which we shall now deriue?[88]

Puttenham, referring to the names of the figures of rhetoric, explained

> . . the straungenesse thereof proceedes but of noueltie and disaquaintance with our eares, which in processe of tyme, and by custome will frame very well.[89]

Others preferred to define words when they were first introduced, as when Elyot appended to the word *circumspection*, 'whiche signifieth as moche as beholdynge on every parte'.[90]

Since the employment of the vernacular had been intended primarily for the benefit of the uneducated, and since nationalistic spirits were high in England, there was naturally a certain amount of antipathy to foreign importations. Sir John Cheke, the purist, presented the extremist view in 1561,

> I am of this opinion that our own tung shold be written cleane and pure, vnmixt and vnmangled with borowing of other tunges.[91]

The main objection, however, would appear to be one against affectation rather than against judicious borrowings, as Sir Thomas Wilson remarked in 1553,

> The folie is espied, when either we will vse such wordes as fewe men do vse, or vse them out of place, when an other might serue much better.[92]

There were those whose patriotism respected words of native provenance, though they were employed mainly in the realm of poetry. George Gascoigne confessed this preference

> . . I have more faulted in keeping the olde English wordes (quamvis iam obsoleta) than in borrowing of other languages,[93]

and Spenser's annotator attributed the supposed inadequacy of the vernacular to the neglect of the native elements

> . . in my opinion it is one special prayse, of many whych are dew to this Poete, that he hath laboured to restore, as to theyr rightfull heritage such good and naturall words as haue ben long time out of vse and almost cleare disherited.[94]

Such employment of older words Philemon Holland in 1600 ascribed to his patriotism,

> Wherein, if I have called againe into use some old words, let it be attributed to the love of my countrey language.[95]

Others commended using existing elements and modifying their signification by employing prefixes and suffixes and by compounding. Arthur Golding said

> . . great care hath been taken, by forming and deryuing of fit names and termes, out of the fountaynes of our own tongue, though not altogether most vsuall, yet alwaies con-

ceyuable and easie to be vnderstood;[96]

It was Peter Heylyn's opinion that the vernacular was

neither so boistrous as the Germane, nor effeminate as the French; yet as significant as the Latine, and farre more happie in the conjunction or union of many words together.[97]

Ralph Lever claimed in THE ARTE OF REASON, 1573

. . As for deuising of newe termes, and compounding of wordes, our tongue hath a speciall grace . . The cause is, for that the moste parte of Englyshe wordes are shorte, and stande on one sillable a peece . .[98]

The study of Rhetoric was another means used to embellish the tongue. Thomas Nash in THE ANATOMIE OF ABSURDITIE 1589 referred to it

Amongst all the ornaments of Artes, Rhetorike is to be had in highest reputation, without the which all the rest are naked, and she onely garnished.[99]

The great English rhetorics of the century – and there were many – gave a stimulus and granted consent to the creation of new words. As Gladys Willcock has said 'The vernacular rhetoricians, like the great army of translators, have the common end of the *défense et illustration* of the mother-tongue. They had to guide and assert the capacities of English, not only against the Ancients, but against the Italians and the French. Rhetoric was armament; words and figures were ammunition'.[100]

The vernacular movement in every country was characterised by the compilation of dictionaries. Although the fifteenth century had produced a number of word lists, Sir Thomas Elyot was quick to realize the complete inadequacy of such vocabularies. His was the 'first attempt in the century to compile a Latin-English dictionary commensurate with the needs incident to the new learning'.[101] In 1589 John Rider remarked,

. . considering the great vtilitie of a Dictionarie, whose matter is manifold, and vse generall,[102]

But the spirit of the age demanded more than Latin-English and English-Latin word-books; it called for English dictionaries for the English. In 1582 Mulcaster remarked

It were a thing verie praiseworthie in my opinion, and no lesse profitable then praise worthie, if som one well learned

> and as laborious a man, wold gather all the words which we vse in our English tung, whether naturall or incorporate, out of all professions, as well learned as not, into one dictionarie . .[103]

As a result of such a compilation

> we should then know what we both write and speak: we should then discern the depth of their conceits, which either coined our own words, or incorporated the foren.[104]

Though Dryden claimed later that English did not possess

> so much as a tolerable dictionary, or a grammar; so that our language is in a manner barbarous[105]

many attempts were made during the sixteenth century to supply both needs as the editions of the works of men like Elyot, Cooper, Thomas Thomas, Bullokar and Greaves all amply show. The grammarian was, in a sense, the more successful. The difficulty which faced the lexicographer was that the language was growing so fast. It was not until the turn of the century, when the future of the language was established and when the earlier acquisitions were beginning to take their place in its fabric, that Robert Cawdrey was able to publish the first English dictionary A TABLE ALPHABETICALL in 1604

> . . Whereby they may the more easilie and better understand many hard English wordes, which they shall heare or read in Scriptures, Sermons, or elswhere, and also be made able to use the same aptly themselves . .[106]

But Shakespeare was still writing, and it was not until he had finished with the mother tongue and exploited all its resources that the claim of the adequacy of the vernacular had been endorsed once and for all in England.

I

THE DILEMMA OF THE VERNACULAR

THE political, social and religious upheavals which prefaced the second half of the sixteenth century in Wales produced serious repercussions on the vernacular. Already the Court of the Council of the Marches had introduced anglicizing influences among the Welsh gentry who had come to regard English as the language of preferment; such tendencies were sealed in 1536. The Act of Union, passed in the last session of the Reformation Parliament, provided that,

> all Justices Commissioners Shireves Coroners Eschetours Stewardes and their lieutenauntes and all other officers and ministers of the lawe shall proclayme and kepe the sessions courtes hundredes letes Shireves courtes and all other courtes in the Englisshe Tonge and all othes of officers iuries and enquestes and all other affidavithes verdictes and Wagers of lawe to be geven and done in the Englisshe tonge And also that frome hensforth no personne or personnes that use the Welsshe speche or langage shall have or enjoy any maner office or fees within the Realme of Englonde Wales or other the Kinges dominions upon peyn of forfaiting the same offices or fees onles he or they use and exercise the speche or langage of Englisshe.[1]

The language of government law and administration, therefore, was to be English.[2]

Economic conditions were bringing the countries closer together. Trade was increasing and, as a result, communications improved. The economy of Tudor England was prospering while that of Wales remained relatively poor. When there were new exciting developments in Wales, for example the lead, copper and mining enterprises, they were financed by English capitalists and attracted a steady following of industrial workers from England.

In formal education the Welsh language became inferior. The monastic schools had disappeared, and with the accession of

Henry VIII, Welsh parents had begun sending their sons to Shrewsbury and later to Westminster and other English public schools. The lesser gentry patronized the new Tudor foundations or re-foundations in Wales such as at Abergavenny, Brecon, Bangor, Carmarthen and Ruthin. In such schools, the senior pupils employed Latin and Greek in conversation while the younger boys were allowed English.[3] From these schools, those who wished to pursue their studies went out of Wales to the universities and inns of court and chancery. Such education hardly fostered the native traditions of language and culture in Wales.

Welsh had been imperilled on several occasions before and had reasserted itself with great zest; but there was a particular difficulty attached to the dilemma of Tudor times. Previously there had always been the poets whom Salesbury called '[p]enseiri yr Jaith'[4] and Dr. John Davies 'vetustæ linguæ custodes'.[5] Now it seemed as if the Welsh poetic tradition was in danger of fading out. It was fast losing the patronage of the gentry. But there were other radical causes for its decay; the Renaissance brought with it new literary vogues which tended to challenge the conservative forms of the Welsh bards. Already in the Welsh tradition itself, there were signs of decay.[6]

There were also the exacting claims of the Renaissance and Reformation, the union of which demanded that all should share in the fruits of learning. Such a challenge, however, proved to be the means of victory for the Welsh language. The problem which this dissemination of knowledge created was being faced by devotees of other modern vernaculars, and the young Welsh humanists, either in their studies at Oxford, Cambridge, or the Inns of Court, or in their journeys on the Continent, had witnessed such devotion. They returned to Wales with a missionary spirit both for Protestantism and for the language. Soon the Welsh Roman Catholics joined the battle for the vernacular and for the claims of the Holy See.[7] Both sides were acutely conscious of their social obligations.

Sir John Prys, himself conversant with the contents of medieval manuscripts of instruction and devotion, realized the need for their diffusion,

> Ac er bod y rhain gyda lhawer o betheu da erailh yn yskrivennedic mewn bagad o hen lyfreu kymraeg, etto nyd ydy yr lhyyfreu hynny yn gyffredinol ymysk y bobyl.[8]

– a sentiment echoed again and again in the prefaces of the period. Gruffydd Robert was so impressed with the value of Morys Clynnog's ATHRAVAETH,

> ni eḷais ar fynghalon na pharụn i brintio: fal y gaḷo eraiḷ syḍ ag eissie y cyfryụ ymborth ysprydol arnynt, fod yn gyfrānol o'r ụleḍ a darfu ichụi i harlụy . .[9]

In 1595 Henri Perri stated

> nas darbhu geni nebun idho ei hun, namyn yn hytrach iw wlad, iw bhro, iw genetl, iw rieni, a'i garedigion . .[10]

and William Morgan won the gratitude of Huw Lewys,

> am iddaw ddwyn y cyfryw drysawr, sef gwir a phurlan air duw, i oleuni yn gyffredinawl i bawb, 'rhwn ydoedd or blaen guddiedic rhag llawer, . .[11]

At the turn of the century, Thomas Wiliems extended the labour of his vocabulary collecting to his fellow countrymen,

> nys galhwn ag ny dhylywn gadw'n briotol ymyhun y peth a dhylei vod yn gyphredin y laweroedh o herwydh y mowrles a'r budhiant, . . a dhaw ag a dyf o honaw.[12]

Such social consciousness together with respect for the native tradition was in the end to secure sufficient regard for the vernacular to render it useful and even eloquent. Humanism and Religion won the day for Welsh; they had become the foil to the Act of Union of 1536.

Had the people become acquainted with Latin or English, the dilemma occasioned by the Renaissance and Reformation would have been resolved. Latin was still essentially the language of learning, it was 'copiosa molto, e ornatissima',[13] and as Thomas Wiliems put it,

> . . Lhatin, sydh gyphredinaf iaith yn holh Europa[14]

In 1575, Rudolph Waddington had expressed

> how necessary the knowledge of the Latine tongue is to any of us, that eyther desire to be entred into other bordering tongues or to serch the depth of any Science, or the assurance of our saluation through the true understanding of holy scripture, is so cōmonly knowne, and so generally agreed on, that happie seemes he that may attaine therto,[15]

Richard Owen had lamented the lack of it in 1552,

> Minau pan gevais im llaw y llyver hwnn o waith Mayster Lewys Vives ai ddarllain drosto mi a ddamunais yn vy meddwl vod y merched yn ddyscedic o ladyng ymhob gwlad.[16]

Many of the works of learning, of the liberal arts and sciences were being translated into English, and the output of polemical literature and instructive writings in that tongue was considerable. In 1587, Dafydd Johns referred to

> . . Saesnaec, yn yr hon y mae yrowan bob celfyddyd wedi gosod allan yn berffaith,[17]

It was natural, therefore, that concerned as they were with the dissemination of knowledge, many of the Welsh humanists should commend familiarity with English. Salesbury was one of the more ardent protagonists; in 1547, he described English as

> angenrheitiach i ni r Kymbry no neb wrthei er esceuluset genym am y peth:[18]

The DICTIONARY, he explained, was intended

> ir hai hynny yn vnic o chwenychant vegys y dylent vynny kyfrwyddyt i ddarllen a deall iaith Saesnec iaith heddyw vrddedic o bob rhyw oreuddysc iaith gyflawn o ddawn a buddygoliaeth ac iaith nid chwaith anhawdd i dyscy[19]

He expressed his opinion most vehemently in 1550,

> I would fayne wyth all industry endeuer my selfe to helpe and further all Walshemen to come to the knoweledge of Englyshe, as a language moste expediente, and most worthiest to be learned, studied, and enhaũced, of al them that be subiectes, and vnder the obeysaunce of the imperiall diademe, and triumphante Sceptre of Englande, euen for the attaynement of knowledge in Gods word, and other liberall sciences whyche thorowe the benifite of the learned men of our dayes be communely hadde and sette forth in the said Englishe tongue.[20]

As a result of his commending English on the one hand, and his arduous efforts to preserve Welsh on the other, Salesbury has become something of an enigma in Welsh scholarship. The most plausible explanation of these two seemingly contradictory elements has been presented by Mr. W. A. Mathias, 'Yr oedd W.S. eisoes wedi bod yn Rhydychen ac fe wyddai am y llyfrau Saesneg o bob math yr oedd ysgolheigion y cyfnod yn Lloegr yn eu cynhyrchu, . . [a'r] Ysgrythur . . gwaith araf oedd cyfieithu a chyfansoddi, a gwyddai W.S. nad oedd obaith i'r Cymry gael yr Ysgrythur a'r llyfrau eraill yr oedd cymaint o'u hangen arnynt am rai blynyddoedd. . . Daeth i'r casgliad mai'r unig beth amdani oedd gwasgu ar y Cymry i ddysgu Saesneg *er mwyn iddynt ddod i wybod am air Duw ac ymgydnabyddu â dysg newydd y Dadeni*, ac aeth ati i baratoi'r Geiriadur'.[21]

Such an explanation, however, is inadequate, and the full understanding of Salesbury's attitude and that of many of his contemporaries may only be sought in the fact that they were truly Tudor Welshmen.[22] It was part of the political behaviour of the humanist to accept the dictates of 'il principio', and Salesbury and his fellow Welshmen were no exceptions. For him and for them 'llywadraeth kalon brenhin' was 'drwy law ddew'.[23] Absolutism demanded uniformity, and Salesbury applauded Henry VIII for having established English as the overall language of the realm,

> . . Wherby youre Royalmes and dominions haue receaued infinitte cōmodyties and auoyded greate displeasures and disturbaunce whyche bothe nowe disquiet other Royalmes and before your graces tyme hath also vexed thys your Royalme of Englande: your excellēt wysdome (as you haue an eye to euery parte and membre of your Dominion) hath causede to be enactede and stablyshede by your moste cheffe & heghest counsayl of the parlyament, that there shal herafter be no differēce in lawes and language bytwyxte youre subiectes of youre principalytye of Wales and your other subiectes of your Royalme of Englande mooste prudently consyderynge what great hatred debate & scryffe hathe rysen emongeste men by reason of dyuersitie of language and what a bonde and knotte of loue and frendshyppe the cōmunion of one tonge is, & that also by the iudgement of all wyse men it is moost conueniente and mete that they that be vnder dominiō of one most gracious Hedde and Kynge shal vse also one lāguage . . Wherfore seyng ther is many of your graces subiectes in Wales that readethe parfytlye, the welshe tonge whych if they had, englyshe expounded in the welshe speche, myght be bothe theyr owne scholemaysters and other mennes also, and therby most spedely obteyne the knolege of the englishe tōge through

> owt all the countraye I haue writtē a lytle englyshe dyctionary with the welshe interpretacion wher vnto I haue prefixed a treatyse of the englyshe pronunication of the letters:[24]

The object of the work was made known in the privilege which granted permission

> to our welbeloued subiectes Williā Salesbury and Ihon Waley to print or cause to be printed oure booke entitled a Dictionarie bothe in englyshe & welche, whereby our welbeloued subiects in Wales may the soner attayne and learne our mere englyshe tonge.[25]

The Act of 1563 which commanded that the Bible and Prayer Book should be translated stated that the Welsh editions should be accompanied by the English Bible and Prayer Book in all churches so that the people might 'by conferring both Tongues together the sooner attain to the knowledge of the English Tongue'.[26]

Such attainment, however, was looked upon as 'adeiladu cestill yn yr awyr'[27] and the immediate concern was a didactic one; the exigency of the issue was regarded in retrospect by George Owen in 1594,

> . . nowe not three yeares past wee haue the light of the ghospell, yea the whole Byble in o^r^ owne natyue tounge wch in shortt tyme must needs worke great good inwardly in the hartts of the people, whearas the seruice and sacraments in the English-tounge was as straunge to many or most of the symplest sorte as the masse in the tyme of blyndness was to the rest of England,[28]

The report on *Welsh in Education and Life* would claim that scholars employed Welsh as a last resort;[29] recent scholarship has revealed, however, that in the case of Salesbury, this is true only in so far as it refers to his religious works. In 1547, Sir John Prys said

> pechod mawr oeḋ ado yr sawl mil o enaideu y vyneḋ ar gyfyrgolh rac eiseu gwybodaeth y fyd gatholic, ac y syḋ heb wybod iaith yny byd onyd kymraeg.[30]

He compiled his primer,

> er kadw eu henaidieu, y rhai ny alho enilh kyfrwyḋyd rhagorach drwy ieithoḋ erailh, y peth y ḋymynwn ydyn y geisiaw yn dyfal.[31]

It was Salesbury's opinion that Scripture was necessary in the vernacular,

> er mwyn y cyniuer ohanoch or nyd yw n abyl, nac mewn kyfflypwriaeth y ddyscy Sasnaec.[32]

In A TREATISE CONTAINING THE AEQUITY OF AN HUMBLE SUPPLICATION, John Penry described to the Queen and the Parliament the condition of the Welsh people and justified preaching in the vernacular,

> The woorde in welsh neither must nor can bee gotten. Must not, because al should be brought to speak English, of the condition the trueth were made knowen vnto them, I would it were brought to passe. And shal we be in ignorance vntil wee all learne English? This is not hir Maiesties will wee are assured. Raise vp preaching euen in welsh, & the vniformity of the language wil bee sooner attained. . . Cōsider Anglisey, Mamgymrû Caernarûon, & see if all these people must dwel vpon mount Gerizzin and be subiect to the curse, because they vnderstand not the English toung.[33]

The most balanced presentation of the whole problem was given by William Morgan in his EPISTOLA DEDICATORIA in 1588,

> Siqui consensus retinendi gratia, nostrates vt Anglicum sermonem ediscant adigendos esse potiùs, quàm Scripturas in nostrum sermonem vertendas esse volunt: dum vnitati student, ne veritati obsint cautiores esse velim, & dum concordiam promouent, ne religionem amoueant, magis esse solicitos opto. Quamuis enim eiusdem insulæ incolas eiusdem sermonis & loquelæ esse magnopere optandum sit: æquè tamen perpendendum est, istud vt perficiatur tantum temporis & negotij peti, vt intereà Dei populum miserima illius verbi fame interire, velle, aut pati nimis sit sæuum atque crudele. Deinde non dubium est, quin religionis quàm sermonis ad vnitatem plus valeat similitudo & consensus. Vnitatem præthereà pietati, vtilitatem religioni, & externam quandam inter homines concordiam eximiæ illi paci quam Dei verbum humanis animis imprimit præferre, non satis pium est. Postremò, quàm non sapiunt, si verbi diuini in materna lingua habendi prohibitionem, aliena vt ediscatur quicquam mouere opinantur? Religio enim nisi vulgari lingua edoceatur, ignota latitabit.[34]

In 1595, Morris Kyffin explained,

> pwy ni wyr mor amhossibl fydde dwyn yr holl bobl i ddyscu

Saesonaeg ag i golli eu Cymraeg; ag mor resynol yn y cyfamser fydde colli peth anneirif o eneidieu dynion eisieu dysc a dawn iw hyfforddi?[35]

Many writers related the sinfulness of the people to lack of instruction in the vernacular; in 1551 William Salesbury remarked on the misery of his fellow countrymen,

Tum demum si qna eodem loco, eadem tribu natorum miseria me tangeret: qui procul dubio quamuis sacre scientie rudes deum (si qui alii) ardent si dicerem me quid curasse illud Apostoli tam tremendum quam ueredicum, Quod si adhuc uelatum est Euangelium nostrum, in his qui pereunt, uelatum est &c.[36]

and in the petition believed to be his, he advanced a further remedy,

for the expulsment of sooch miserable darknes for the lack of the shynyng lyght of Christe's Gospell as yet styll remayneth among the inhabitantes of the same principalitie . . that then it may please your good lordships to wyll and require and com'aund the learned men to traducte the boke of the Lordes Testament into the vulgare walsh tong . .[37]

Gruffydd Robert, in 1568, referred to the dearth of works of instruction,

E fyḍ tostur fynghalō pā feḍyliụyf faint syḍ o blant trụy dir cymru . . yn methu, ag yn cymryd ḷụybr ānụyiaụl eisiau cael oi mebyd i hyphoḍi meụn dysc, ai meithrī meụn moessaụl gāpau. Yr achos fụyaf o hynn yụ diphig ḷyfrau a draethant o'r cyphelib ystyr.[38]

and Thomas Johns spoke of the plight of the Welsh people prior to the translation of the Bible,

heb ddysk heb ddim heb ddoniay syw, heb lifr düw yn athro heb ddyscediaeth gwir gan neb, mawr oedd ddallineb kymro.[39]

As late as 1595, Huw Lewys was still able to lament the paucity of didactic literature,

y diffig hwnn o lyfreu sy in mysc . . yw yr achos paham y mae cymeint o anwybodaeth mewn pethau ysprydawl in mysc:[40]

In his AD LECTOREM PRAEFATIO of 1632, John Davies asserted that the end of language was to communicate the great works of God to the people,

> alij, quo Magnalia Dei popularibus suis (qui præcipuus est linguarum omnium vsus) linguâ quâ nati sunt promptiùs enuncient;[41]

It was only a century earlier that printing had been employed to make such communication possible. Ieuan ab Wiliam ap Dafydd ab Einws lamented the fact that whereas books were being printed in England, in Wales it was still the lot of the copyists to attempt to disseminate works of instruction; it was his contribution to compile a book between 1544 and 1552

> ar i gost i hyn i gael o bobyl ddifyrwch o hono a lles yw heneidiav.[42]

In 1581 John Foxe had referred to

> that inestimable benefit of Gods blessing, prepared for the behoofe of his Church, I meane the singuler and most excellent Art of Emprinting.[43]

John Prys had also regarded it as a providential and propitious discovery,

> Ac yr awr y Rhoes duw y prynt yn mysk ni er amylhau gwybodaeth y eireu bedigedic ef, iawn yni, val y gwnaeth holh gristionogaeth heb law, gymryt rhann or daeoni hwnnw gyda yn hwy, val na bai diffrwyth rhod kystal a hon yni mwy noc y erailh,[44]

and the author of a collection of englynion in 1563 asked for a blessing on this new means of dissemination in Welsh,

> y tad ar mab mad amen
> ar ysbryd diasbri i berchen
> a lwyddo wrth brintio ar bren
> brvtaniaith loywiaith lawen[45]

All these factors made translation unavoidable, and the primary necessity was Scripture in the vernacular, as Sir John Prys realized,

> Am hynny gwedys yw rhoi yngymraec beth or yscrythur lan, o herwyd bod lhawer o gymry a vedair darlhein kymraeg, heb vedru darlhein vn gair saesnec na lhadin, ag yn enwedic y pynckeu y sy anghenrheydiol y bob rhyw gristion y gwybot dan berigyl y enaid,[46]

In the same year Salesbury declared

> Ac ny vynwch ymado yn dalgrwn dec a fydd Christ, . . mynwch yr yscrythur lan yn ych iaith, . .[47]

The official approval for Scripture in Welsh came in April 1563 when Salesbury's 'long desired peticion'[48] was answered, and the Queen consented to an Act ordaining that

> the whole Bible, containing the New Testament and the Old, with the Book of Common Prayer and Administration of the Sacraments, as is now used within this Realm in English, be truly and exactly translated into the British or Welsh tongue[49]

Works of instruction were also needed. In 1633, David Rowlands explained,

> Peth arferedig yw cyfeithio a throi gweithredoedd duwiol gwyr da defosionol o r naill iaith i iaith arall er chwanegu gwybodaeth, er egorud deall, ac er pureiddio moesau da ac arferau christianogaidd,[50]

But the value of translation had been realized earlier; Morris Kyffin was conscious of the output in other countries,

> mi a welaf bob peth, . . ymhôb iaith yngHred, mor bybyr, ag mor berffaith, drwy ddysc a diwdrwydd gwyr da, nad rhaid iddynt (yn ei herwydd) wrth ddim ychwaneg. O'r tu arall, prin y gwela 'i ddim (onid llyfr Gair Duw'n vnig) yn y Gymraec, a dim ffrwyth rhinwedd ynddo, i ddyscu ag i hyfforddi yr rhai annyscedig.[51]

Huw Lewys listed his reasons for translating Coverdale into Welsh and,

> Y 3 achos yw, tlodi ac eisieu gwlad Gymbru o lyfreu yn i hiaith ei hun, ir diwedd ar defnydd hwnn, sef, er rhoddi iachusawl, ac ysprydawl ddiddanwch, ir sawl sydd glwyfus, . . A chyd bae bob gwlad a theyrnas o'n hamgylch, a llyfreu duwiol, daionus ganthynt, yw dyscu yn ffordd yr Arglwydd, ac yn ffydd Grist, yn ddigonawl, eto prin y cawsom ni lyfreu, (yr hynn sydd drwm a gofidus gennyf) yn ein iaith ein hun, in athrawy yngwyddorion, ac ymhyncieu cyntaf y ffydd.[52]

When he wondered how best he might serve his fellow countrymen,

> . . ni fedrais ddychymig, na dyfeisiaw vn modd gwell, nac wrth roddi allan, ryw draethiad dduwiol, neu lyfr dyscedig, ymhwy vn y cae fy anwyl gydwladwyr, y Cymbru, yn ei tafodiaith ei hun, iachusawl, ac ysprydawl athrawiaeth, a dysceidiaeth.[53]

One of the principal aims of the humanist was to convey learning to the prince's court; it had been elaborated by Castiglione in his IL CORTEGIANO. Learning had become the desideratum of the age and many Welsh scholars wished to set up a cultured society in the Renaissance sense of that expression. Salesbury, addressing 'Iohn Edwardes of Chyrcke' in 1550 remarked,

> I know well that you stamer some what both in the Laten tonge, and in this science also,[54]

which was the occasion for his translation THE DESCRIPCION OF THE SPHERE OR FRAME OF THE WORLDE. It was his opinion that

> a ny bydd dysc, gwybodaeth doethineb, a dywolwch mewn iaith, pa well hi na sirmwnt adar gwylltion, . .[55]

Earlier, the translator of the TRACTATUS DE ARMIS had remarked upon a lack of learning in Welsh compared with other languages,

> Ac am hynny gweddus a r[r]eidiol oedd i bob gwr bonheddic urddasol o genedlaeth Gymry wybod yr arwyddion a berthynai iddo y'w dwyn yn ddieniwed i bawb, a medru i dosbarth a'i disgrio yn iaith Gymraeg megis mewn ieithoedd eraill, r[r]ac myned y gelvyddyt honn ar arveu hevyt ar gyveiliorni ymysg y genedlaeth megis y mae yn debic o eissieu ymarver ohoni yn iaith y Bryttanieid ar ni bont ddysgedic mewn ieithoedd eraill;[56]

By 1562, Richard Eden was able to claim that English had become

> enriched and amplyfied by sundry bookes in manner of all artes translated owt of Latine and other toonges into Englysshe.[57]

and as early as 1547, Salesbury had been aware of such learning in English,

> iaith heddyw vrddedic o bob rhyw oreuddysc iaith gyflawn o ddawn a buddygoliaeth.[58]

This awareness made more marked the shortcomings of the Welsh language,

> Ef wyr llawer Nasion y saith gelfyddyt, or ny chlypu er oed o ywrth Christ. Ny wyddoch chwi er ech ehud cymmendot, nag vn gelfyddyt perfeith, na dim yn iawn ddilwgyr o fydd Christ.[59]

Richard Davies lamented the fact that Wales was not partaking of the greater light of the Renaissance,

> Mawr ywr goleuni a ddoeth ir byt, a' mawr i cynyddodd ac i chwanegawdd pob celfyddyt, a' gwybodaeth sprytawl, a

> corphorawl, ym hob iaith ym hop gwlad, ac ym hop teyrnas ir pen ddychmycwyt celfyddyt Printio. Eithr mor ddiystyr fyday iaith y Cymro, a chyn bellet ir esceulusit, ac na allodd y print ddwyn ffrwyth yn y byt yw gyfri ir Cymro yn i iaith i hun hyd . . Wiliam Salsburi . . a' Syr Ihon Prys . .[60]

Referring to the diffusion of knowledge as part of the plan of God, he remarked,

> mawr fu eu drugaredd yn eyn amser ni ofewn y trugain mhlonedd hynn: o herwydd llawer o genadau dyscedic, a' phrophwydi nerthawl ym hob dysceidiaeth, celfyddyday, ieithoedd a gwybodaeth ysdrydol. Trwy waith yrhain i may oll teyrnasoedd Cred o fewn Europa eysus wedi egoryt eu llygait, . . Etto . . nit wytti'r Cymro gyfrannoc o ddim hapach or golenni mawr hwnn sy tros wyneb y byt. Can ys nit escrifennodd ac ni phrintiodd neb o honynt ddim yn dy iaith di.[61]

Gruffydd Robert had witnessed the learning in other countries,

> Canys nyd oes nag ystori i ḍyscu henafiæth, na chylfyḍyd o enụ, a ḷes, na gụybodæth o ḍim, a dalai i ḍysgu nas darfu i'r hyspaniaith, phrangeg, a'r eidaliaith i tanu, ai hau ymysc gụyr i gụlad,[62]

In his own language he found nothing

> meụn scrifen a phrụyth ynḍo i hyphorḍi meụn dysg, a daụn[63]

Siôn Dafydd Rhys was also aware of this learning,

> o's golygwch' arr genedloedh a' phobloedh erailh, megys y Groecieit, a''r Lhadinieit; chwi a 'elhwch ganbhod, nadd oes nebryw 'wybôdaeth na chelbhydhyd dann yr haul, o'r a dhichon bôd mywn dyn, na's capher ei gweled yn amlwc ynn eu hiaith a'e' lhybhreu hwy, yn gyn amled, a' bôd holh Europa yn gybhlawn o 'i hiaith a''i lhybhreu hwy, . . A' gwedy yr hain hynn, y dilynassant yr Ieithoedh cyphrêdin, megys yr Italieith, yr Hyspanieith, y Phraghec, yr Almannieith, y Saesônec, y Scotieith, a' ieithoedh erailh heb law hynny,[64]

The position gave much concern to the humanists in Wales, and it became their earnest endeavour to correct it. Morris Kyffin had little time for those who pursued what he regarded to be the trivialities of language,

> Eisieu dysc a duwioldeb, ag nid eisieu llythyrēneu i adrodd

> dysc, sydd ar yr iaith gymraeg.[65]

In his dedication to Wiliam Meredydd, he referred to the DEFFYNNIAD as

> cyfieythiad hyn o addysc[66]

In 1567, Gruffydd Robert affirmed that with the proper cultivation of the language,

> mi a obeithiaf, cyn nemaur o ennyd y gụelir o'mgụaithí ymysg y cymru laụer pụnc o ḍysg, a gụybodaeth ni eḷais moi ḍangos iḍynt hyd yn hynn.[67]

In Western Europe 'learning' connoted the 'sapientia' enshrined in the works of the Ancients. In Wales it appropriated an extra meaning; Welsh humanists looked back with pride to the traditions of native learning, and it became their concern to salvage it. Such learning had reached its ebb; as Mr. W. A. Mathias has said, 'Cyfnod tywyll yn hanes y llsgrau. Cymraeg oedd y blynyddoedd oddeutu 1545, a bron na ddywedwn ei bod yn argyfwng ar ddysg Gymreig'.[68]

Salesbury referred to the dilemma,

> oh, howe it greaueth me to disclose the vnfayned trueth, and to confesse the vndisimuled veritie, that there remayneth now but walsh pamphlets for the goodly Brytish bokes, sometyme so well furnished wyth all kynde of literature: and so few Brytyshe fragmentes of the booke of Christes owne religion remaine vnwormeaten, and defended from iniurye of tyme, and the booke of Howel da ap Cadell so longe preserued salfe and sounde?[69]

Siôn Dafydd Rhys showed concern not only to protect such learning, but also to print it,

> A phaham na's galhant Pendebhigion a' Bonhedhigion Cymry hwynteu hebhyd, beri casclu yghhyd, a' phrintiaw eu petheu odidoccabh hwytheu . . y Pribheirdh . . y Posbheirdh . . yr Arwydhbheirdh, . . hyd yn y beym nî ynn galhu yn 'wastad bhôd . . ynn ymdhybhyrru ynn eyn Hiaith a''n petheu cymreic; yn gystal a'r Saeson, a' Chēhedloedh erailh yñ eu Lhybhreu a'e' petheu hwynteu.[70]

Difficulties did not disappear when the use of the vernacular had been justified. The sixteenth century bequeathed to the modern languages the problem of equipping themselves to express ideas which, hitherto, had been communicated in Latin. It was the process of exact translation which made obvious the difficulties, as Gruffudd Bola had observed two centuries earlier,

> Vn peth hagen a dylyy ti wybot ar y dechreu pan trosser ieith yn y llall megys lladin ygkymraec. na ellir yn wastat symut y geir yn y gilyd. a chyt a hynny kynnal priodolder yr ieith. a synnvyr yr ymadravd yn tec. vrth hynny y troes i weitheu y geir yn y gilyd. A gveith ereill y dodeis synnvyr yn lle y synnvyr. Hervyd mod. A phriodolder. yn ieith ni.[71]

Thomas Bedingfield remarked on the same difficulty when translating into English,

> For although some men suppose it an easie thing, to reduce the conceipt of anie author into another language; yet am I assured it behoooueth him not onelie to haue an exact vnderstanding in that toong, wherein the author writeth, but also apt words, and fit phrases in his owne, to expresse the same.[72]

And when it is remembered that, for example, out of a total of forty-three known Anglican works produced during the years 1558–1633, thirty-five were translations,[73] and that translation demanded

> [d]dodi gair tra gair, ag i bob gair rhoddi ei enw anianol, megys y bydd rhaid wrth gyfieithu a throi peth o vn iaith ir llall:[74]

it is not surprising that the deficiencies of the vernacular became obvious to writers of the period. Despite the fact that there was a tradition of learning in Wales, the habit of writing learned works had waned in 'the outworne baren Britishe',[75] and, in any case, many of the new ideas ushered in by the sixteenth century demanded brand new significants. The author of the treatise on heraldry, which belongs to the fifteenth century, had experienced difficulty in translating technical terms,

> . . am vod iaith Gymraec mor anaml na cheffir ohoni ddigon o eirieu perthynol i'r gwaith newydd hwnn, . .[76]

Morris Kyffin explained the greater difficulty of translation than of original composition,

> Hefyd, rhaid i ti wybod na ellir cyfieuthu dim o iaith arall yn gymraeg, cyn rhwydded, a chyn rhydded, ag y dichyn vn scrifenny'r peth a ddychmygo ag a fynno fo'i hun.[77]

There is no lack of remarks on the inadequacy which writers found in Welsh in the sixteenth century, though one needs to be circumspect in evaluating such evidence. Several writers of the early century in England were deploring lack of learning in their vernacular when William Salesbury was speaking of English as 'vrddedic o bob oreuddysc'.[78] Nevertheless, it is estimated that most of the remarks concerning Welsh, found in the prefaces and dedications of the period, relate fairly honestly the feelings which writers had towards the vernacular.[79]

In some cases, the inadequacy of the Welsh does not necessarily reflect the intrinsic lack of the language, any more than Salesbury's remark,

> I wyll therfore, wrest it rather than truely tourne it, and that for lacke of farther connynge, . .[80]

reflected the inadequacy of English. It would be incorrect, for example, to regard Welsh as being inadequate merely because of the poverty of Rowland Puleston's language or Siôn Conwy's vocabulary. Some writers apologized for being unequal to the task of translation. Richard Owen prefaced his translation of Vives in 1552 with

> a lle nid oedd gennyf i ddygon o gymraec gedwch vi yn escussodol: mi ai rrois mal i gellir i ddallt yn sathredic.[81]

Robert Gwyn expressed a similar sentiment in 1574,

> A mine heb fedry onyd yn bring ymodi mo'm tafod nag y ddywedyd y Gymraeg fel y dylwn, na chwaith yn medry ysgrifeny yn gywir gimint ag y fedra y dywedyd, . . heb fedry dangos hanner fy meddwl ynGhymraeg iawn fel y dylwn, . .[82]

Rhosier Smyth in his RHYBYDD excused his inadequacy,

> na ryfedda dim dienc llavver o faiau yn y llyfran yma nid yn unig yn yr orthograph: eythr hefyd yn y cyfiaithiad, . . canys bvvm allan o'm bro a'm gvvlad yspaid daugain mylynedd . . heb gael haiach o o gyfeddach gyda chymro yn y byd. heb na llyfr na modd arall i'm helpu[83]

On the whole, Salesbury's remarks on the vernacular were consistent. His most balanced opinion, though slightly non-committal, was given in 1550,

> Agayne as for the Walsh tong euen as it is not now to be compared wyth the Englyshe language, so is it not so rude, so grosse, nor so barbarous, as straũgers beynge therein all ignorante and blynd do adiugde it to be: nor yet (to speake indifferentlye wythout all affections) is it not all so

copious, so fyne, so pure, nor so fully replenished with eligancie, graces, & eloquence, as they them selues suppose it.[84]

In his treatise on Rhetoric, translated from Mosellanus, he referred to the mother tongue as

yr iaith sydd yn kychwyn ar dramgwydd.[85]

In 1567 he used the familiar terminology of English writers of the earlier sixteenth century,

The matter I acknowledge to be but base, the tongue to be but obscure . .[86]

Gruffydd Robert explained how it was natural that the language should appear inadequate when the demands were new,

na fid diystr, na diflas gennyt, fyngụeled i yn ymḍangos mor ḍisas, ag mor āhylụybr, canys hōn yu'r aụr gyntaf yr amcanụyd fynụyn i lụyhr celfyḍyd.[87]

When the treatises of the arts and sciences would be translated,

e fyḍ caledi maụr pan geissier cyfieuthu a trhoi yr vnrhiụ hethau i'r gymraeg, am fod yn brin y geiriau gēnym, erbod yr iaith o honi ihum cyn gyfoethocced ag un araḷ.[88]

The spoken language had deteriorated from the standards of the literary language,

am fod yr iaith gyphredin wedy ei chymyscu a llawer o eirieu anghyfieith sathredig ymhlith y bobl, a bod yr hen eirieu ar wir Gymraeg wedy myned ar gyfyrgoll ai habergofi.[89]

There was a large element of English words in the language, though in 1595, Morris Kyffin contended,

Hawdd yw gwybod am ryw eiriau seisnig, nad oes, ag na bu er ioed eiriau cymreig iw cael;[90]

The inadequacy became most marked in the translation of religious works. In 1547, Salesbury explained how the language of daily usage was completely insufficient for the demands of Scripture and the Arts,

A ydych chwi yn tybieit nat rait amgenach eirieu, na mwy amryw ar amadroddion y draythy dysceidaeth, ac y adrodd athrawaeth a chelfyddodeu, nag sydd genwch chwi yn arueredic wrth siarad beunydd yn pryny a gwerthy a bwyta ac yfed? Ac od ych chwi yn ty byeit hynny voch tuyller.[91]

The author of the DRYCH was conscious of the difficulty of transferring the nuances of religious terms,

Ag yn enwedig wrth gyfieithu r Scrythur lan a geirieu r

> Saint rhaid yw bod yn bryderus i geisio geiriau cyfaddas cynhwynawl i henw pob beth. Gwir iawn yw hynn oll pan fytho dyn yn cyfieithu ag yn trossi r Scrythur lan i iaith arall, ag yn ei dodi ai gossod allan i ddynion yw darllain yn enw Scrythur laan: Yna y bydd rhaid ymchwel bob gair yn gymhwys ag yn ei briawd anian cyd bo tywyll i lawer:[92]

William Morgan did not claim that Welsh had not possessed the necessary significants for the translation of Scripture, but he maintained that such terms had either become obsolete or lost,

> verba quibus Brytannicè explicanda erant quæ in Scripturis sacris sacra tractantur mysteria, vel Letheis quasi aquis deleta prorsus euanuerant, vel desuetudinis quodam quasi cinere obducta atque sepulta iacuerant,[93]

It may be concluded that as it stood, Welsh was unequal to the demands of the moment. When Gruffydd Robert examined, to the best of his ability and his material at hand, the possibilities of the traditional twenty-four metres, he adjudged them insufficient to treat of

> ryụ ḍefnyḍ hir, amlbarth, ne . . ystori o hir amser,[94]

He gave it as his opinion that in such circumstances,

> ef a eiḷ barḍ enụog, . . fod yn fodlon, i'r fath fessurau y mae'r eidaluyr yn i arfer.[95]

To many of the writers of the day, the range of the language seemed to be as circumscribed as the twenty-four metres appeared to Gruffydd Robert, and quite insufficient to express properly the new ideas which were rapidly filling the minds of men. Scholars differed merely in the ways in which they sought to solve the problem.

There were obvious reasons for this inadequacy. The religious revolution demanded translation of the whole of the Scripture and the Liturgy; the amount of religious work in the vernacular was small. The range of material to be translated was much wider than ever before, and the invention of printing brought all authors under the scrutiny of a larger audience than the most popular medieval manuscript could command. This was John Baret's thought in 1573,

> But I both vnwilling, and halfe ashamed to haue our rude notes come abrode vnder the viewe of so many learned eyes, . .[96]

The increased facilities of education and interest in both classical and modern languages made readers more critical. Where the works were translations of Scripture, so much depended on the interpretation of terms, that exact signification was a fundamental concern.

But scholars in Wales in the sixteenth century cited other reasons for the inadequacy of the language, and the chief one was that it had lost its prestige as a result of the neglect of the upper classes, for as the author of the DRYCH put it,

> Py baei r bonheddigion Cymreig yn ymroi i ddarllen ag i scrifennu eu hiaith, hynny a wnaei i r cyphredin hefyd fawrhau a hophi r iaith.[97]

There were those who would hasten its end, as Siôn Dafydd Rhys noted,

> . . a' sylhu ohonobh' hebhyd, bhôd gelynion yr iaith ym mronn cáel eu gwynbhyd arnei:[98]

The culmination of anglicizing influences had come with the Act of Union when Welsh lost its official status and regard for the vernacular for patriotic reasons was diminishing. Salesbury asked in 1547,

> Oh y pa peth ydd yngeneis i am wladwriaeth, can na ys gwyr Kymbro heddyo o pa han yw gwladwriaeth.[99]

Such a feeling of inferiority among speakers, appropriately termed by Professor T. J. Morgan as 'dolur ysbrydol'[100] caused alarm among those humanists who wished to see Welsh taking its place among the other languages of Western Europe. The earliest reference to such 'dolur ysbrydol' was made by Gruffudd Hiraethog,

> A phob vn o'r rhai a dariont nemor oddi kartref yn kashav ac yn gillwng dros gof jaith i ganedic wlad a thavodiad i vam gnawdawl.[101]

Gruffydd Robert deplored the disesteem of the language,

> VRth fyngu̦eled fyhun, er ysl̦auer o flynyad̦oed̦, heb bris gan neb arnaf tru̦y dir cymru, . .[102]

and

> E fyd̦ u̦eithiau'n dostur fynghalon u̦rth veled l̦auer a anu̦yd ag a fagu̦yd im doedyd, yn d̦iystr genthynt amdanaf, tan geissio ymu̦rthod a mi,[103]

To the author of the DRYCH, the effect of such disregard went deeper than neglect; it undermined the respect which the language might otherwise have gained from English people,

> Ag fal i mae r Cymbry ymhell oddiwrth ddaioni, felly y mae r bonheddigion ag eraill yn ysgluso ag yn diystyru r iaith gymraec: Am fod y rhann fwyaf or bonheddigion heb fedru na darllain nag yscrifennu cymbraeg: Y peth sydd gywilydd iddynt: A hyn sydd yn peri ir Saeson dybieid a doydyd fod yr iaith yn salw, yn wael, ag yn ddiphrwyth ddiberth, heb dalu dim: Am eu bod yn gweled y bonheddigion Cymbreig heb roi pris arnei: Canys pe y baei r iaith yn talu dim, y Saeson a dybygent y gwnai r bonheddigion Cymreig fwy o bris arni, nag i maent yn i wneuthur. Hefyd chwi a gewch rai or Cymry mor ddiflas ag mor ddibris ddigywilydd, ag iddynt ar ol bod vn flwyddyn yn Lloegr, gymeryd arnynt ollwng eu Cymraeg dros gof, cyn dyscu Saesneg ddim cyful i dda. Y coegni a r mursendod hyn yn y Cymry sy yn peri ir Saeson dybied na thâl yr iaith ddim, am fod ar y Cymry gywilydd yn dywedyd eu hiaith i hunain: A hynny a wnaeth ir iaith golli a bod wedi ei chymyscu ai llygru a Saesneg.[104]

Morris Kyffin observed the same attitude among the religious leaders of the people,

> chwith iawn yw dal sylw ar lawer o wyr Eglwysig cymreig yn byw ar bris eneidieu dynion, a bagad eraill o Gymry yn cymeryd arnynt eulun dysc a goruchafiæth, heb genthynt fri'n y byd a'r iaith eu gwlad, eithr rhusso'i doedyd, a chwylyddio'i chlywed, rhag ofn iss-hau ar eu gradd a'u cymeriad; heb na medry darllen, na cheisio myfyrio dim a fae a ffrwyth yntho'n gymraeg, . .[105]

Humanists regarded it as their duty to demonstrate to the younger scholar gentlemen who were becoming increasingly anglicized that Wales possessed a dignified language, learning and literature of which they might well be proud. They claimed that it was lack of this realization and respect for such a tradition which was undermining the potential rights of the vernacular. Other modern languages were being respected and cultivated, and it was in this contrast that Gruffydd Robert saw the reason for the insufficiency of Welsh,

> ụedi ymy gerḍed o fraiḍ benn yr hyspaē trụy phrainc, Phlandria, ag Alemania, a'r Eidal hyd yn eithaf Calabria tan ymofyn ymhob ḷe am gyflụr, braīt, a helynt yr ieithoeḍ

syḍ tu draụ i hynny, ni fedraisí ụeled, na chụaith gloụed oḍiụrth yrụn; na bai yn cael gụneuthur yn faụr o honi ymysc paub, syḍ o naturiæth yn i doeḍyḍ. Ag ụrth fod pob vn o honynt yn cael i'mgeleḍ, ai pherchi gē i phohl, hithau drachefn i ụneuthur iaụn, am y caredigrụyd a gafoḍ sy'n traethu iụ phobl bob peth, a fo gụiụ i ụybod; hyfryd i gloụed, a gogoneḍus i ụneuthur. . . Pan ụelais innau hynny, e fu ryfeḍ iaụn gēnyf, fod y cymru morḍiḍarbod amdanaf;[106]

In 1592, Siôn Dafydd Rhys maintained that Welsh remained uncultivated among the vernaculars of Western Europe,

NYd oes nemor o iaith . . ynn Eurôpa a'"i hynysoedh, na's cabhas ei hymgelêdhu a'"i choledh gann ei Ieithydhion a'"i Gwladwyr 'ihûn o amser i gilydh; onyd eyn hiaith ni y Cymry.[107]

Welsh humanists asserted that their language had once been a language of learning, but the vocabulary of such learning had been lost either by the passage of time and the disappearance of manuscripts,

. . am vyned iaith gamberaec mor esgevlvs ymae arwydd ar gadwriaeth y llyfrav, mor anaml i kair dim yn gwbl yntynt heb ddarn yn eisiav, . .[108]

or by the conservatism of the poets who had been from time immemorial the 'custodes' of the history, language and traditions of the Welsh.[109] By the late fifteenth century, the religious houses in Wales had declined, and by the time of their final dissolution, much of the preserve of learning which had been in their possession for centuries, had been lost. Many of the humanists implored for the return of such manuscripts in order that their vocabulary might be utilized again. Such was Salesbury's plea in 1547,

Ac och ddeo . . na byddei cynniuer ar a vedd oll Cembry o lyfreu or iaith . . wedy r lladrata or modd hynny. Ac e vyddei haws i Cembro ddeall y pregethwr, wrth pregethy gair Deo. E vyddei haws o lawer, ir prechethwr traythy gair Deo yn ddeallus, Ac a vyddei haws i wr dyscedic o Cambro wedy bod yn hir allan oe wlad, ac anghynefino ar iaith, cyfieithy iaith arall, ar iaith einym. Ac am hynny atolwg y chwy nyd er vy mwyn i, anyd er mwyn Deo, nyd er pleser na serch arno vi, anyd er carat ar ddeo, er lles ych eneitieu ych hunein, er tragyvythawl glod ywch (y sawl ae gwnel) . . pop vn o hanawch ys ydd yn meddy nac y perchenogy llyfreu n y byd o iaith Camberaec, attolwg ew cludo at pwy ryw sawl Gymbry pynac a vo hyspys genwch i bod yn darbod yn naturial tros ymgeledd gwladwrieth yr vnryw iaith.[110]

The dearth of older documents made Salesbury's project of translating the Scripture more difficult,

O bleit o ran ych bod chwi yn darguddio hen lyfreu ych iaith, ac yn enwedic y rei or yscrythur lan, nyd bywr Cembro er dyscedicket vo, a veidyr iawn draythy r yscrythur lan y chwy yn Camberaec, can y bregnach ar y priniaith ydd ych chwi yr oes hon yn gyffredin.[111]

Humanist scholars in all countries realized that dictionaries were essential as stores of ready words required by original writers and translators. Welsh could only become adequate when such a work could be compiled with the aid of older material,

y gadw'r iaith einom, . . yn dragyvyth,[112]

Thomas Wiliems deplored

y Cymru anvrytaneidh, . . a chanthunt hen lhyurae Cymraec alhasent wneuthur lhes y mi ag y'w gwlad, ag er hynny nyt hepcorent dhim o honunt, ond eu dyrngudhio, eu murnio a'u celcu, heb wneuthur dim lhes na budh vdhunt eu hunein . . na'i cyfranu a'r sawl a vedrasai o dhywrthynt, . .[113]

Some looked further back; earlier disasters in the history of Wales had resulted in the loss of native literature. Richard Davies commented on this in 1567,

galw ith cof y gollet a gavas y Cymru am eu llyfray beth bynac faynt, ay celfyddyt, ay historiae, ay Achay, ay Scrythur 'lan: ys llwyr ir anrheithiwyt oll Cymru o honynt. Can ys pan 'oystynget Cymru tan goron Loygr trwy nerth arfeu, diammay ddistrowio llawer oy llyfray hwynt yn hynny o trin. . . Pa destriw ar lyfray a gavas Cymru o ddiwrth rhyfel Owain Glyndwr, hawdd yw i ddyall wrth y trefi, Escoptae, manochlogydd, ar tem'leu a loscwyt trwy oll Cymru y pryt hynny.[114]

Humphrey Lhuyd in his COMMENTARIOLI BRITANNICAE DESCRIPTIONIS FRAGMENTUM, published in 1572, referred to the learning and the books which the old Welsh church possessed; such learning, he declared, had been destroyed by Augustine, 'monasteria et bibliothecas vastabant' and 'monachos viros doctissimos delevisse'.[115]

The poets were also blamed for the dilemma in which the humanists found the Welsh language. They had jealously guarded the preserve of the past and made no attempt to enhance the vocabulary to meet the changing modes of the time. As far as evidence goes, Gruffudd Hiraethog would appear to have been the only 'pencerdd' who championed the cause of the vernacular in the manner of the humanists. Siôn Dafydd Rhys reproved the poets,

> y Prydydhion, wrth bhôd yn gymeint eu hawydh i geisio cadw dirgelion a' rhinoedh yr Iaith a'‘r Brydydhiaeth ynn eu plîth e'hûnain, . . ebh a dharbhu idhynt nyd yn vnic dhibha‘r Iaith a'‘r Brydydhiaeth, onyd hebhyd colhi eu hên Bhraint, . .[116]

Recent research, however, has revealed that the basis of Rhys's criticism can be justified only in part; nevertheless, the stringency of the bardic discipline tended to stifle the language from developing as fully as it might have done. The paradox was that the language of the poets became the foundation for the literature of succeeding centuries.

Despite their concern with the new problems facing the vernacular, and the shortcomings which such demands detected, the humanists were not without belief in the future of Welsh. In 1567, Gruffydd Robert remarked,

> mi a obeithia o hynn aḷan trụy nerth duụ, athrylith, diụdrụyḍ a gụiụ fyfyrdod fynghymru cariadus, y byḍ genthyn nhụy fụy o serch i mi, a chan innau fụy o ḍiḍanụch a golud idynt hụythau: oblygyd hynn yḍụyf yn adolụg i bob naturiol gymro dalu dyledus gariad i‘r iaith gymraeg:[117]

II

BELIEF IN THE VERNACULAR

MANY of the humanist scholars in Wales believed wholeheartedly in the intrinsic potentialities of the vernacular, and since by 1560 the contents of many hitherto scattered and probably unexamined manuscripts had become better known, they were able to substantiate their claims by references to the copiousness of the older vocabulary. Even in England, where regard for the past accomplishments of the language played only a very minor part in the battle for the mother tongue, Richard Sherry claimed,

> It is not unknowen that oure language for the barbarousnes and lacke of eloquence hathe bene complayned of, and yet not trewely, for anye defaut in the toungue it selfe, but rather for slackenes of our coũtrimen, whiche have alwayes set lyght by searchyng out the elegance and proper speaches that be ful many in it:[1]

Such 'searchyng out' however, belongs more properly to the vernacular movement in Wales. There, detailed examination of the various redactions of the laws would be sufficient to convince them of the niceties of which the language was capable.

It was evidently Salesbury's knowledge of the Welsh manuscripts which prompted him to describe in 1550 the copiousness of the vocabulary,

> . . what select wordes, what consonant and fine termes, and what sentencious and net adages, whych the olde, sage, & learned fathers haue not only inuented, but also of the Grekes and the Latines moste prosperouslye haue taken, translated, accepted, and vntill thys daye stil retayned:[2]

John Penry, while conceding to the greater desirability of English for the purposes of Christian teaching, found Welsh as adequate as other vernaculars,

> But why can we not haue preaching in our owne toung? Because the minister is not able to vtter his mind in welsh. He maie. For wee haue as manie words as in any vulgar toung whatsoeuer and we might borrow from the latine &c[3].

Siôn Dafydd Rhys referred to 'perpheithrwydh ac odidawgrwydh eych Hiaith', and explained how, with proper cultivation, it would be possible to

> arwain iaith morr odîdoc ac morr brydbherth, ac yw y Gymráec, alhan o'r dygn dywylhi y mae hî yndho, a''i dwyn idh ei hên berpheithrwydh a''i theilyghdawd gynt.[4]

Morris Kyffin was able to applaud the Welsh of two contemporary writers, commending not only the purity of their language but also its eloquence,

> Yn-nhal y Testament hwnnw y gwelais i lythyr duwiol dyscedig at y Cymry, o waith y gwir barchedig Dâd Richard Escob Meniw . . yr hwn lythyr a scrifennodd . . mewn Cymraec groyw, hyfedr, ymadroddus, . . Heblaw hynny mi a welais ddosparth byr ar y rhan gyntaf i Ramadeg cymraec a brintiesid er ys-talm, yr hwn sydd ddarn o waith dyscedig ynghelfyddyd gramadec, mor buraidd, mor lathraidd, ag mor odidawg ei ymadroddiad, na ellir damuno dim perffeithiach yn hynny o beth.[5]

Gruffydd Robert was more extravagant in his claims; he not only asserted its potentialities by the side of other vernaculars 'nid ydynt ụeḷ i braint no minnau' in these words,

> . . minnau mor ḷaụnḷythr im scrifēnu, cyn gyfoethocced o eiriau, cyn hyned fynechreuad a'r falchaf o'r ieithocḍ a hēuais.[6]

but alleged that if Welsh were properly cultivated, it would surpass other languages,

> Ond pe caniadai ḍuụ amser cymụys i fyned trosdynt unuaith drachefn ag megis i falu yn fan y cheirch, a ḍarfu ini i fras silio, mi a obeithiụn y gaḷḷem amlhygu odidoụgrụyḍ yn-niaith, a gyrru blys ar ụyr yn gụlad iụ dyscu ai'mgleḍu, a gụneuthur cyụiliḍ i'r ieithoeḍ estronaụl oi hamgylch, er maint i cymheriad, ai parch ymysc y saụl syḍ yn i medru.[7]

The author of the DRYCH elaborated upon this,

> Ond i mae gan y fi beth amcan ar ieithoedd eraill, a pheth gwybodaeth o rann yr iaith Gymraec: ag yn wir wrth gymharu ieithoedd ynghyd ny wela fi yr un or ieithoedd cyphredin eraill, nad yw r Gymraeg yn gystal ar oreu o honynt oll, os ceiph ei dodi a i gossod allan yn ei rhith ai heulun i hun, ie ag yn blaenori ar lawer o ieithoedd ereill mywn aml foddau a fedrwn eu henwi, ag a wyr y Cymbro dyscedig.[8]

– echoing the sentiments of men like Alberti, Tory, Henri Estienne and Carew in their several countries.

The strength of the belief in the antiquity and renown of the British enabled writers both to feel proud of their native heritage and to regard with respect, earlier periods in the development of their language. This latter element brings them into sharp contrast with many of their counterparts in the other countries of Western Europe. In France, du Bellay advised the poets of the Pléiade to turn away from

> toutes ces vieilles poesies francoises . . et autres telles espiceries qui corrompent le goust de nostre langue et ne servent sinon á porter tesmoignage de nostre ignorance.[9]

In England, not until the beginning of the seventeenth century did the Saxon origin of English bring prestige to their tongue, because although Sir Thomas Smith spoke of the Saxons as those

> from whom our tongue is deriued to this day[10]

such a thesis bore no real connection with the movement for the embellishment of the vernacular.[11] But in Wales, the position was quite different.

The accession to the throne of one of Welsh blood gave new encouragement to the British cause, and the sixteenth century with its interest in the past promoted it further. The vogue of Brutus the Trojan had waned in the fifteenth century, but there was a revival. As Sir T. D. Kendrick has explained, 'This revival was in a large measure due to the outbursts of patriotic enthusiasm that followed the accession in 1485 of the Welshman, Henry Tudor, to the throne'.[12]

In 1587, Morris Kyffin addressed the Queen,

> A Blessed Branch of Brutus Royall Race;
> To Brytish wightes a Blisfull worldly ioy,
>
> . . . .
>
> Ye Bryttish Poets, Repeat in Royall Song,
> (With waightie woords, vsde in King Arthurs daies)
> Th' Imperiall Stock, from whence your Queene hath sprong;[13]

and in 1603, Thomas Salisbury spoke of

> yr amser bendigedig hwnn pann rôddes Duw i ni ardderchawg frenin yr hwn sydd yn dyfod o lîn Brutus (er an-

rhaethawl ddiddanwch oll gywir-galon frutaniaid).[14]

Professor Glanmor Williams has said of the Welsh humanists, ' . . they gave the Established Church a strongly patriotic appeal not only by the successful use of the vernacular in worship, but also by creating a version of early British history which represented the Reformation as a restoration of the Church of the Golden Age of their British forebears and so a consummation of the whole Tudor claim to have vindicated the messianic prophecies of a thousand years'.[15] Mr. Saunders Lewis has claimed that the Protestant Church thesis was based upon the theory of the distinction of the British.[16] To the Protestants, the distinction of being Welsh was not merely a matter of antiquity; they claimed that the British embraced Christianity at the beginning and held it purely. Richard Davies treated this fully in 1567,

> vn rhinwedd ragorawl . . ath harddai gynt, ac a rodday yt ragorfraint a goruchelder, sef crefydd dilwgr, crystynogaeth bur, a ffydd ffrwythlon ddiofer. . . yddym yn gwelet cael or Brytaniait Crefydd Christ yn ddilwgr ac yn perffaith. . . gwir grefydd Christ, a gair Duw a hardday y Brytaniait gynt, . .[17]

This theory was widely held by Protestant historians in the sixteenth century; it was derived in the main from Geoffrey of Monmouth and from Gildas where scholars found reference to the Scripture once available in Welsh. Tyndale had made reference to it, and Archbishop Matthew Parker's DE ANTIQUITATE BRITANNICAE ECCLESIAE . . and his preface to the larger Bible were distinguished and influential contributions to the thesis. Mr. Lewis has alluded to Salesbury's 'wrth y darlleydd Camberaecgar' which introduced OLL SYNNWYR PEN . . in 1547 as the manifesto of the Renaissance and Protestant humanism in Wales.[18] In it, Salesbury implored the people,

> mynwch yr yscrythur lan yn ych iaith, mal ac y bu hi y gan ych dedwydd henafieit yr hen Urytanneit.

As has already been stated, the magnum opus was Richard Davies's EPISTOL . . . , where the writer declared the tragedy of the dearth of Scripture in the vernacular,

> . . pop gwlat . . yn awyddus ac a mawr groeso yn derbyn gair Dyw . . y mae yn dra salw genyf dy welet ti wlat Cembru, a vu ryw amser gyntaf, yr owrhon yn dyvot yn

olaf ynghyfryw ardderchawc oruuchafieth a hynn: . . Coffa'r hen amser, ymofyn ath henafiait, chwilia'r 'storiay, ti a fuost gynt anrhydeddus, ac vchel dy fraint.[19]

The Bishop preferred reasons for claiming that the Scripture once existed in Welsh, 'perffeithrwydd ffydd y merthyron', the testimony of Eusebius, and,

may cenym ni yn Gymraeg amryw ymadrodion a' diharebion yn aros fyth mewn arfer a' dynnwyt o berfedd yr scrythyr 'lan, . .[20]

The pertinence of such a theory to the question of the vernacular in Wales has been suggested by Professor A. H. Dodd, 'In *The Obedience of a Christian Man*, which appeared just before Davies took his Master's degree, Tyndale defends the English language against the charge of being "too rude" to serve as a vehicle for the word of God; but if English was going to claim parity with the learned tongues, how much stronger the claims of a language spoken among Christians here when Saxon was still a pagan *patois*, and preserved in its purity by bardic schools through all the intervening years!'[21]

John Leland was probably the first to claim that the Welsh poets were the direct descendants of the Druides,[22] and the idea took firm hold on the minds of the young Welsh humanists. Reading the BELLUM GALLICUM of Caesar and the ANNALES and the HISTORIA of Tacitus, they found reference to the Druides and details concerning them; Caesar referred to their existence in Anglesey. Sir John Prys, following Leland, also claimed that the Welsh poets were the natural heirs of the Druides, and as a result, the bardic tradition could be traced back to the pre-Christian era; in fact the Druides and the Bardi (also mentioned by Caesar) sang at the same time as the poets of Greece and Rome. Wiliam Midleton in his ANNERCH . . remarked of Welsh grammar,

Com. lib. 6.

a chan dhwedyd o Jul. Cæsar y bydhai y Drudion gynt vgain mlynedh yn dysgû y gelfydhyd honno:[23]

Lodowicke Lloid, in his commendatory verses to Henri Perri, coupled the names of the bards with the writers of great antiquity,

IF of their Thalmud Iewes made much, if Turks
their Alcoran boast,
If Priests of Egypt did commend their Memphia

Chronicles most:
Then Brittaines may their Bardi brag, and yeeld
them gwerdon due;[24]

It was the widest claim that the distinguished Benedictine, Périon, could make for French, that it was derived from Greek,

> Ioachimi Perionii Benedictini . . DIALOGORUM DE LINGUAE GALLICAE ORIGINE, EIUSQUE CUM GRAECA COGNATIONE, LIBRI QUATUOR, Paris, 1555

and even that assumption was qualified by his admitting a substantial Latin influence. Geoffrey of Monmouth in his HISTORIA had claimed for Welsh equal antiquity and status with Latin, Greek and Hebrew. In 1621, John Davies asserted that Welsh was one of the chief languages of the world, spoken when tongues were ordained at the Tower of Babel.[25] As a result, it had greater prestige than continental languages which were considered to be impure and mixed. In his DICTIONARIUM DUPLEX of 1632, Davies paid attention to what he regarded as cognate Hebraic forms. It was such noble origin which prompted Salesbury to remark on the similarity between Hebrew and Welsh idiom,

> In Matheo multum addictus fui cōtextui Hebraico: non q aspernatus Grecū, sed q Hebraica phrasis propius ad nostrā accedit.[26]

and which allowed Perri, in his discussion of the figures of speech, to use classical and Welsh examples indifferently.

As a result of these theories of antiquity, Welsh humanists in the sixteenth century were eager to adopt British as the correct name for their mother tongue. Salesbury discussed the misnomer in 1550,

> And bycause . . I do not entend to encourage you nor anye man els, than is oner desierous to the studye of Brytyshe (I meane the language that by continuall misnomer the recorder of the aunciente hostilitie is called Walshe) I wyll not once speake a a worde in praise of it (thoughe and if I were learned I myght say somewhat to it).[27]

Humphrey Lhuyd assured his readers that,

> They are not therefore to be credited which denie the Welsh to be the old Brytish toong[28]

For the benefit of those historians who knew no Welsh, he intended

> to entreate a lytle of the knowledge of the Britysh tongue[29]

and he listed

> Certayne Welsh, or rather true British woordes, . .[30]

In his laudatory verse prefacing Perri's EGLVRYN PHRAETHINEB, R.V. sang

> CARMEN ENCOMIASTIchon in laudem Britannicæ Linguæ & operis.

Robert Holland, in his epistle before his translation of BASILIKON DORON in 1604, referring to the Welsh as

> A Nation of great antiquity, keeping their countrey, and contynuing their language so long a tyme inuiolate without change or mixture.

decided

> to translate into the true Brittish tongue, your Highnesse Instructions to your dearest sonne, . .

Thomas Salisbury alluded to

> . . a'r ôr-hên-iaith Gymraeg[31]

and in a letter written by him to Sir John Wynn of Gwydir, spoke of

> . . your proverbs ye psalmes and many good trea[tyses] of mr Perkynnes wth other good thinges in ye brittishe tounge . .[32]

The Welsh humanists regarded the British as being not only ancient but also renowned. Nothing concerned them more than the learning which the older stages of their tongue possessed. They knew that from the days of Taliesin, the language had been associated with the court, and furthermore, they asserted that it had remained pure. Humphrey Lhuyd explained how

> the works of Merdhyn and of Taliessin, who wrote aboue 1000. yeares past, are almost the same words which they vse at this daie . .[33]

Sir John Prys spoke at length of how the bardic discipline had inherited the Trivium and the Quadrivium,

> Posteriorum verò post annos abhinc quingentos scripta multò dilucidiora sunt tum lectu tum intellectu, & plurimum lucis prioribus afferunt. Atque vt nullum erat tempus, quo huiusmodi literati inter eos non reperiantur, sic nullum penè doctrinæ genus est cuius non habent principia & canones quasdam generales sua lingua descriptas. Quia prętex Grammaticam (quàm vt dixi habent exactissimam)

> Rhetoricæ, & Dialecticæ, Geometriæ insuper & Arithmeticæ regulas habent generales, & de Astronomia pariter & Cosmographia complures habent commentarios, quibus eorum vates plurimum studij adhibuisse, ex eorum carminibus liquet. In Physicis & re medica habent quamplurima ad methodum tradita. In sacris etiam literis habent etiam nonnulla pręsertim compendij in morem desumpta, quæ vel ad historiæ cognitionem, vel ad morum compositionem sufficere videbantur: Leges insuper quibus municipes olim vsi sunt, ante sexcentos annos, . . Denique quod maximè ad rem de qua agitur spectat, historias habent tum productiores & fusas, tum breues & contractas chronicorum in morem sua lingua descriptas, . .[34]

In 1550 Salesbury referred to the copiousness of the older vocabulary and the learning to be found in the vernacular,

> Howebeit whan the whole Isle was commune ly called Brytayne, the dwellers Brutes or Brytōs, and accordyngelye their language Brytishe, I wyll not refell nor greatelye denye, neyther can I iustelye gaynsaye but theyr tonge than was as copious of fit wordes, and all maner of propre vocables, and as well adournated wyth worshypfull sciences, and honorable knoweledge, as anye other barbarous tonges were.[35]

Richard Davies mentioned

> aurhydedd bydol yr hen Brytaniait . . y amryw gylfyddyday hwynt, synwyr, dysc, doythineb,[36]

Welsh was not lacking in 'sapientia', though as William Salesbury, Richard Davies, Humphrey Lhuyd and John Davies explained, much of the oldest records of such learning had been lost; as Thomas Johns put it in his CERDD DDIOLCH AM Y BEIBL CYMRAEG,

> hen historiay a llifray da, pwy bynag ay darlleno,
> ve gaif gweled ymhob hynt, vod kifarch gynt ar gymro.
>
> pob kelvyddyd a dysc ffraeth, ddoedd gwir wybodaeth ganto
> nes y Scolan gythrel gay, ddinistro llyfray r kymro.[37]

Salesbury was conscious that the distinction of Welsh letters had now been interrupted, but he found compensation for such a loss in the fact that other great nations had suffered a similar fate,

> But considering that other nations, as the Hebrewes, the Grekes, and the Romaines, who ruled all the world, haue sustained such alteracion of language, such translation of countries, such inuasion by alientes, shall not we than the posteritie of the old Britons, being neuer but a handful, in comparison of the least of any of those forenamed people, be well content to suffer the lyke?[38]

It was the opinion of later writers that Welsh had been providentially preserved. Thomas Salisbury felt that the vernacular had been safeguarded by

> y Gor-uchaf Dduw . . eusus ers Seith-gant a'r-higain o flynyddoedd a rhagor, y mysc cyn-niuer o droyadau ar fyd,[39]

and this was reiterated by Edward Kyffin,

> . . eyn hiaith . . yr honn a ddeffynnodd y Goruchaf dduw yn yr vn-lle yn y deyrnas honn ers seith-gant-a'r-higen o flynyddoedd ag y chwaneg ymysc cyn-niuer o amrafaelion Genhedloedd, terfyscoedd a dinistroedd a fu i'n mysc er yr amser hwnnw i geisio difa a dinistrio yr iaith ai phobl yn llwyr.[40]

Thomas Wiliems expressed the same sentiment in the preface to his TRYSAWR YR IAITH LATIN AR GYMRAEC,

> . . er cadw . . y Gymraec loewlan byth bythoedh ag hyt dhiwedh y byt val y mae'n gobeith ar Dhuw a'i cadwodh mor rhyuedh yn dhisothach dhigymmysc, ag yn dhilwgr er ys mwy na dwyuil a seithgant o vlynydhoedh ymysc cymeint a chyniuer o ieithoedh estron wledydh,[41]

A factor less profound than 'belief' in the language was that Welsh remained the only language spoken and understood by 'the most and greatest number of all her Majesty's most loving and obedient subjects inhabiting within her Highness Dominion and Country of Wales'.[42] And as Professor W. Ogwen Williams has remarked, 'The bards certainly made no mean contribution towards saving the language from deterioration . . In a society such as that of Tudor Wales where Welsh was the sole language of most of the people, native folk lore, poetry and song must also have played their part in sustaining the mother tongue. . . The ordinary rank and file minstrels, harpists, storytellers, and lesser bards of Tudor Wales, unlike their Irish brethren, plied their craft freely in fairs and markets, in alehouses, and in the homes of the people. They must have helped, albeit unconsciously, in ensuring the survival of the language'.[43]

But it was belief in the language among the leaders of society which was to secure its future. It is little wonder that with the prestige of the Welsh running so high, scholars were prepared to devote untiring energy to the nurture of the vernacular.

III

THE EMBELLISHMENT OF THE VERNACULAR

IN A letter written to Siôn Dafydd Rhys, Wiliam Midleton reveals an interest in language which is usually associated with the later antiquarians,

> newyddyon nyt oes gennyf onyt ysgyfarn yn iaith gernyw yw clust yn iaith ninav[1]

Such a remark, however, is typical of the interest in language which characterized the sixteenth century. Professor A. H. Dodd has referred to the 'antiquarian and philological zeal'[2] at Oxford where so many of the younger sons of the old Welsh families were finding themselves. Already the universities, where concern previously had been solely with Latin, now introduced Greek and Hebrew into their curricula. Printing, the increased communication with other countries, and the new emphasis on the interpretation of the Bible all accelerated such preoccupation with language, and convinced scholars of the inadequacies of their own vernaculars. In 1533, Sir Thomas Elyot declared,

> I intend to augment our Englyshe tongue, wherby men shulde as well expresse more abundantly the thynge that they conceyued in theyr hartis (wherfore language was ordeyned) hauynge wordes apte for the pourpose:[3]

Whatever were the opinions of the past glories of the language, Welsh scholars realized that it needed embellishment and respect to render it adequate to express the new ideas of the Renaissance and Reformation. Salesbury asserted in 1547,

> A chymerwch hyn yn lle rybydd y cenyf vi: a nyd achubwch chwi a chweirio a pherfeithio r iaith kyn daruod am y to ys ydd heddio, y bydd ryhwyr y gwaith gwedy.[4]

Mr. Saunders Lewis would interpret this, 'Troi'r Gymraeg yn iaith llys, dyna ystyr achub yr iaith a'i chweirio a'i pherffeithio',[5] but despite the fact that setting up a courtly society in Wales was undoubtedly part of the intention of the Welsh humanists, on the whole it would appear that the phrase had a less profound signification. Scholars saw that the spoken language had deteriorated far from the literary standards, and that if it were to keep apace with the other modern vernaculars in designating new concepts to 'expresse more abundantly the thynge that they conceyued in theyr hartis', then it must be embellished. The primary intention of the author of the DRYCH was to instruct, but,

> ef a gymerir fann arall i goledd ag i ymgeleddu r iaith,[6]

Other countries had already been dealing with the problem, as Siôn Dafydd Rhys noticed,

> A"r ieithoedh hynn olh a gybharbhûant o amser i amser a' Ieithydhion, a' Ieithymgeledhwyr hawdhgârabh o'r byd, ac ewylhysgârabh i ymgelêdhu, a' choledh, a' mawrháu bôb vn o honynt ei iaith 'ihûn; hyd ynn y diwedh, nadd oes cymeint ac vn hedhiw o'r holh ieithoedh cyphrêdin vchod, na bô yndhei holh gelbhydhôdeu'r byd, . .[7]

In contrast, Edward Kyffin found the remedy,

> WRth weled mor ofalus ydiw ieithyddion eraill am ei gwladiaith, . . Pa faint mwy y dylem-mi ymgeleddu eyn hiaith eyn hunain . .[8]

It was necessary after the Act of Union and the slow anglicizing processes of the past to regain morale for the Welsh language. As in other countries, this could best be achieved when the leaders of society themselves decided to patronize the vernacular. The author of the DRYCH observed,

> Py baei r bonheddigion Cymreig yn ymroi i ddarllen ag i scrifennu eu hiaith, hynny a wnaei i r cyphredin hefyd fawrhau a hophi r iaith.[9]

In Italy, the princes took the lead, in France, the courtiers, and in Wales the gentry, those who moved to London and those who remained at home. In Italy, Gelli believed that a sign of some importance in the augmentation of the vernacular was that it was being employed by 'i principi e gli uomini grandi e qualificati' to express profound matters,

> Si può . . agevolmente far coniettura da le cose che sopravengono, che abbia a farsi più ricca e molto più bella . . L'altra è il cominciare i principi e gli uomini grandi e qualificati a scrivere in questa lingua le importantissime cose de' governi de gli Stati, i maneggi de le guerre e gli altri negozi gravi de la faccende, che da non molto in dietro si scrivevano tutti in lingua latina. Perchè, non vi date a intendere

che una lingua diventi mai ricca e bella per i ragionamenti de' plebei e de le donniciuole, che favellan sempre . . di cose basse.[10]

The last sentence recalls similar remarks by Salesbury in 1547,

A ydych chwi yn tybieit nat rait amgenach eirieu, na mwy amryw ar amadroddion y draythy dysceidaeth, ac y adrodd athrawaeth a chelfyddodeu, nag sydd genwch chwi yn arueredic wrth siarad beunydd yn pryny a gwerthy a bwyta ac yfed?[11]

Perri would have men write of 'le importantissime cose' in Welsh, and Clynnog's letter containing 'negozi gravi' was written in the mother tongue.[12] The Earl of Pembroke, the 'anrhydeḍussaf bennadur' of the Welsh language, and its 'dibaḷ noḍed',[13] would appear to have been the hereditary example of 'l'uomo grande' who favoured his country speech. Wiliam Llŷn extolled him,

Pe bai r iarll pybyr i win
Oll ger bronn Lloegr ai brenin
Doedai ef a di difar
Gymraec wrth Gymro ai gar.[14]

Gruffydd Robert praised him in similar fashion,

Canys e ụyr hoḷ gymru, a ḷoegr faint ych serch i'r fruttaniaith, pryd na ḍoedech ụrth gymro, ond cymraeg, ie, ymysg penaduriaid y deyrnas: . . A bid diau gēnych . . fod callon pob gụir Gymro yn crychnneittio yn i gorph o ụir laụenyḍ, pan gloụo ụr o'ch anrhydeḍ chụi, yn doedyd i iaith:[15]

It was Gruffydd Robert's opinion that it was the protection and study by members of the upper classes which accounted for the apparent superiority of other languages,

nid ydynt ụeḷ i braint no minnau: ond cael o honynt imgeleḍ, ai moụrhau gan bennaduriaid, a boneḍigion i gụlad.[16]

The praise of such men was continued by Thomas Wiliems,

Y Gwyrda hynn ny bu'n anwiw ganthunt, ag nyt yw, dreuthu'n eglur dhiletiaith ag yn lhawnlhythyr a dywedyd ag scriuenu iaith eu gwlad mal y gwnai'r adhurnedicaf Wiliam Iarlh Penvro, . . fydhlonaf gyngIhorwr cynniuer vrenhinoedh a brenhinesae Lhoegr, a lhygat holh Gymru, yr hwnn ny phlychiai arno ag ny 'mattaliai 'mysc goreugwyr y Deyrnas adrodh iaith ei vam . .[17]

Another distinguished patron of the language was Sir Edward

Stradling,

> prif ymgledhwr ein iaith Gymraec yn neheuwlad Gymru,[18]

His was substantial patronage, as his will illustrates,

> Whereas there were printed at my expense twelve hundred and fifty British grammars, I do give fifty of them ready bound to my friend Mr. Doctor Davys, the author of them; and my will is, that the rest of them shall be given and bestowed from time to time by my cousin, Sir John Stradling, upon such gentlemen and others as he shall think fit, for the advancement of the British tongue.[19]

Salesbury acknowledged the service of other men,

> Master Richard Longford o Drefalyn, Master Humfre Lloyd o Ddynbych, a Master Jankyn Gwyn o Lan Idlos . . y rei er maint y sy genich o bybyr wybyddiaeth mewn amryw jaithoedd eraill, nid yw chwi . . nag yn tremygv dywodit yr jaith, na chwaith yn anwiw genych ei hiawn eskryvenv, a'i hachvp rrag hi mynet val ydd aeth Britanneg Kernyw yn yr ynys hon, a Brytannaeg Brytaniet Llydaw yn y tir hwnt tra mor, yn llawn llediaeth ag ar ddivankoll hayachen.[20]

Huw Lewys explained how it would be profitless to dedicate his work to one who had no regard for the language,

> ofer fydde i mi, i roddi ef, i vn, sy ddirmygus, a diystyr ganthaw, yr iaith, can's ni ffrisieu ef ynthaw, . .[21]

He paid tribute to Richard Vychan for

> yr vn gamp honn . . sef, bod yn greugar, yn dirion, yn dyner, ac yn naturiol tu-ac at eich gwlad, gann garu, hoffi, perchi, a mavvrygu ych iaith gyssefin eich hun:[22]

So great indeed was the belief in the value of aristocratic patronage, that Robert Holland expressed the hope that King James's son should acquire Welsh,

> . . a taste of the tongue (which he now might easely attaine vnto) would verily hereafter please and satisfie him, as being thereby made able both to speake vnto his people, and also to vnderstand them speaking vnto him, without interpretors, . .[23]

The vernacular gained much from men who felt it was their patriotic duty to use it; Huw Lewys showed such enthusiasm,

> Ac er maint a fu fymhoen yn hynn, er maint oedd ofy chwant, am awydd, i wneuthur, hyd y gallwn, les im gwlad, . .[24]

as did Morris Kyffin,

> er dwyn onof y rhan fwyaf o'm byd hyd yn hyn o'm hoes ym-mhell oddi wrth wlad Gymry, etto wrth fod ymmysc Ieithoedd dieithr, a darfod i mi dreulio f'amser a'm hastudrwydd mewn petheu eraill, ni bu fwy fyngofal ar fyfyrio, a dal i'm cof vn iaith, no'r Gymraec; gan ddamuno allu o honof wneuthyr rhyw lês i'r iaith a'r wlad lle ym ganwyd,[25]

Thomas Salisbury, the stationer, who saw many Welsh books through the press, and whose labours would have produced many more but for the interruption of the Plague, explained the purpose of his work,

> F'Anwyl-gariadus wlâd-wyr, gann fod ynof fawr-wllys ag awydd erioed i lês-hau fyng-wlâd, yr hynn bêth ym-hôb môdd y pen-nodais atto i'r hynn eitha o'm gallu, . . hynny a wnaeth i mi yn ddiweddar gychwyn printio Brutan-aeg drwy obeithio wrth hynny wneuthur i'm gwlâd ryw wasanaeth cymeradwy:[26]

– comparing with the earnest support of the vernacular which Caxton gave in England, and Tory and Robert Estienne in France. It became one of the fundamental elements in the vernacular movement to secure the regard and interest of speakers. Gruffydd Robert declared,

> rhaid ymy ḍamuno ar bob cymro bonheḍig, a rhoụiog, na bo mụy annaturiol i mi, nog yụ pobl eraiḷ i iaith i mammau.[27]

Henri Perri, in a flourish of Rhetoric, urged all Welshmen to love, regard, and improve their native tongue,

> Y dhywedhu, chwchwi bhonedhigion Periglorion, vchelwyr Prydydhion, ac erailh, adolwyn ydhwybh er mwyn cobhadwriaeth henabhieit, er mwyn pwylhedh gwybodaeth er mwyn mawl eich rhieni . . cannorthwywch, jaith y Cymbru, trwssiwch, a diwelhwch, yngystal drwy i chwi 'obrwyo gwyr dyscedic, iw chasclu'n lhwyr rhac dileith anialawg; ei chynnal yn lew, drwy obhal anhepwedh; a'i hardhu 'n bholiannus, . . Ac hebhyd drwy i chwi (bhonedhion) scribhennu yndhi y nailh at y lalh.[28]

Rhosier Smyth repeated the plea in 1615,

> . . anturio y gvvaith yma: . . gan obeithio drvvy hyn, annos a chyphroi y pendefigion a'r penathiaid, i garu i gvvlad, ag i'm gleddu i aith a hefyd y gvvyr dyscedig hybarchys i y scrifenu rhyvv beth tyladvvy er mvvyn budd a lles ivv gvvlad, . .[29]

Another means of embellishing the vernacular was to secure its recognition as a worthy language in the estimation of the educated outside Wales. The sixteenth century witnessed the final ascendancy of the languages of the west as literary media; the novelty of such an ascendancy brought about a desire to spread abroad the potentialities of the vernaculars. In 1521, Barclay wrote a book to teach Englishmen French,

> Here begynneth the introductory to wryte, and to pronounce Frenche.

In 1550, William Thomas compiled

> Principal Rules of the Italian grammer, with a Dictionarie for the better understanding of Boccace, Petrarca, and Dante: . .[30]

Welsh humanists determined to do the same for the prestige of their language, and nothing illustrates better their concern for scholars outside their own country than their historical works. Previously, as in the work of Gutun Owain and Gruffudd Hiraethog, the medium used had been Welsh; now came a change, and the language of the historians became Latin or English. In 1550, Salesbury published

> A briefe and a playne introduction, teachyng how to pronounce the letters in the British tong, (now cōmenly called Walsh) wherby an English man shal not only w^{t} ease read the said tong rightly but markyng ye same wel, it shal be a meaue for him with one labour and diligence to attaine to the true and natural pronunciation of other expediente and most excellente languages[31]

Siôn Dafydd Rhys wished to show abroad the greatness of Welsh poetry and the purpose of his Grammar was,

> . . ceisiaw vrdho Iaith y Cymry, a'e' Cenedl; gann dhangos mywn môdh gwedhus, deilyghdawt a' phrydbherthwch, ac ardherchawgrwydh y Cymry; a' hynny nyd yn vnic i'r Cymry euhûnain, na charbronn nag ynn eu plîth e'hûnain; onyd hebhyd i'r Saeson, ac i dramoredigion Genhedloedh;[32]

which was the point of his writing it in Latin. It is significant that Henry Salesbury in 1593 and John Davies in 1621 chose to show, as did Siôn Dafydd Rhys,

> perpheithrwydh ac odidawgrwydh eych Hiaith chwi a''ch petheu i 'olwc holh Eurôpa mywn Iaith gyphrêdin i bawb;[33]

Humanists in all countries believed that one effective means of enriching the mother tongue was by publishing works of learning in it. Professor R. Foster Jones refers to 'the widely held view that one gauge of the worth of a language is the amount of learning contained in it'.[34] Much of the purpose of the translation of the classics was that in the process, the learning, which originally inhered only in such tongues, might be conveyed to the modern vernaculars and render them eloquent. To the humanist of Western Europe, learning implied one thing – acquaintance with the classical heritage, and there were those in Wales who shared such enthusiasm. There remain, in manuscript, translations from the classics which indicate such interest, as, for example, DYSGEIDIETH KRISTNOGES O VERCH, LLYTHYR ARESTOTELES . . I ALEXANDER MAWR, and LLYFR PRYDFERTH VINCENTIUS LIRINENSIS, . . *a gyfieithwyd o'r Lladin i'r iaith Gamberaec* . .[35] Siôn Dafydd Rhys is reputed to have translated Aristotle's METAPHYSICS, and perhaps it was Gruffydd Robert's express intention of making the tongue sufficiently adequate to render classical writings in Welsh that he compiled his grammar; his part-translation of DE SENECTUTE was his way of demonstrating how such works might be translated. Thomas Wiliems realized how valuable his dictionary would be

> y gyfieithwyr tradoethion pob celuydhyt arbenic o'r gywoethoc Latiniaith y'r geindec Gymraec einom.[36]

In Italy in the sixteenth century the strength of those who championed the vernacular lay in the work of Dante, Petrarch and Boccaccio; Wales, too, had a compelling literary past. In England there were those who looked back with gratitude to the literature of the fourteenth century, but it did not become, as did fourteenth century literature in Italy and Wales, 'a source of general inspiration in the vernacular movement or a fund of so much verbal deposit for utilization in prose' as was explained in the Introduction (page 25). It was the intention of the printer of TOTTEL'S MISCELLANY of 1557 to present fairly recent works in English poetry,

> It resteth nowe (gentle reder) that thou thinke it not evill doon, to publish, to the honor of the Englishe tong, and for profit of the studious of English eloquence, those workes which the ungentle horders up of such treasure have hertefore envied thee.[37]

and such became the desire of Welsh humanists. But they would go back beyond the fifteenth century and publish the works of earlier poets,

> . . peri printio goreuon Lybhreu y Pribheirdh, . . y Posbheirdh . . Ac yn hyttrabh olh, peri casclu hebhyd a' phrintiaw Lhybhreu ac odidogion Gerdheu yr Arwydhbheirdh, . .[38]

Such work would serve a double purpose, it would embellish the tongue and increase its prestige abroad,

> . . yna y buassei Pennadurieit Lhoegr a' Chymru, a' gwyr tramorêdic hebhyd ynn cymrud cymeint o enrhybhêdhod, wrth ganbhod y bhâth degwch ynn yr iaith gymreic, ac ynghhowreindeb a' chelbhydhyd y Prydydhion; ac y byssynt morr chwenychgar i'n hiaith ni, ac ydym ninheu ac awydh i amgobhleidio ac i amgyphred ei hiaith hwynteu;[39]

But neither the translation from the classics nor the copying of work of the native tradition was sufficient in itself to uplift the language; it was the rendering of Scripture into Welsh which achieved that. In Wales it took the place of the Academia della Crusca, of the salons in France and of the universities in England in sanctioning literary usage. What Welsh humanism lost by not publishing translations from the writers of Greece and Rome, it more than gained in the translation of the Bible.[40] Dafydd Johns spoke of the value of Scriptural translation,

> Cowydd i'r glaw ar dryccin ar prinder ai canlynodd: drwy fwrw y bai ar y bobyl am i hanniolch i dduw am i ddaioni ac eisiau i wasnaethu yn well ac eisiau caru i air ef yn i hiaith i hunain, rhwn beth oedd fawr ddedwddwch i gael a lles ir iaith . .[41]

Siôn Dafydd Rhys deplored the condition into which the language had fallen, but

> ynawr yn hwyr ac o bhraidh, a dhechreuodh gaphael pêth gwrtaith gann 'wyrda dyscêdic o'n hamser ni; a' hynny yn enwêdic o rann cymreic-háu corph yr yscrythur lân.[42]

Morris Kyffin and Huw Lewys were also able to estimate the value of the translation of the Bible as far as the language was concerned. Kyffin was critical of Salesbury's rendering, but praised Morgan's translation of 1588, adding,

> Cyn hynny hawdd yw gwybod may digon llesc oedd gyflwr yr iaith gymraeg, pryd na cheid clywed fynychaf, ond y naill

> ai cerdd faswedd, ai ynte rhyw fath arall ar wawd ofer heb na dysc, na dawn, na deunydd ynddi.[43]

and Huw Lewys referred to,

> D. Morgan, (i bwy vn mae holl Gymbru byth yn rhwymedic, nid yn vnic am ei boen ai draul, . . eythr hefyd am iddaw ddwyn y cyfryw drysawr, sef gwir a phurlan air duw, i oleuni yn gyffredinawl i bawb, 'rhwn ydoedd or blaen guddiedic rhag llawer, gann adferu eilwaith yw pharch ai braint, iaith gyforgolledic, ac agos wedi darfod am dani)[44]

Similarly, in 1603, Edward Kyffin discerned its value, acknowledging the wisdom of the Queen,

> yr honn sydd yn canhiadu i ni gael y Scrythur lân yn eyn hiaith eyn hunain, ag oll gyfreidiau eraill ar a ddamunem ei cael tu ag at amlhau Gogoniant Duw, a mawrhâd eyn hiaith:[45]

Apart from the learning which was inherent in classical languages, scholars were impressed by the stability and uniformity which characterized them and they were concerned to introduce a measure of such uniformity into the modern vernaculars. Printing and the dissemination of books made the concern necessary; the result was a great interest in grammar and orthography. For the English, French and Italians, the matter of orthography was an issue of vital importance. In Italy, the second section of Fortunio's grammar was devoted to 'del correttamente scrivere';[46] in France, in 1547, appeared,

> Remarqves svr la Langve Françoise vtiles a cevx qui vevlent bien parler et bien escrire.[47]

In England it received the attention of such distinguished scholars as John Cheke, John Hart, William Bullokar, John Baret and Thomas Smith, whose DIALOGUE CONCERNING THE CORRECT AND EMENDED WRITING OF THE ENGLISH LANGUAGE was published in 1568. Welsh scholars shared this interest, and in the first Welsh book to be printed, Sir John Prys referred to his having changed

> o hen ortograff kymraeg yn amgenach noc y by arveredic escrivenny kynn hynn . .[48]

Salesbury confessed his concern for orthography with an apologia,

> some exclamed, & perhaps meaning well and simply, but sauing correction, though otherwyse learned . . that I had peruerted the whole ortographie of the tounge. Wher in

deede it is not so: but true it is that I altered it very little, and that in very few wordes,[49]

In his grammar, Gruffydd Robert devoted a whole section to orthography which he called 'iaụnscrifenyḍiaeth', a form resembling Fortunio's 'correttamente scrivere' and Mulcaster's 'right writing'. It was part of his project of giving to the language a stability which courtly usage demanded. Morris Kyffin claimed that it was

gormod hyfder mewn vn gwr pwy bynnag fo, yw rhoi allan math newydd ar lytherēneu a scrifennyddiæth, a thybied may cymwys i bawb ei galyn ef.[50]

Nevertheless, Gruffydd Robert found those who, in part, followed his practice, Morys Clynnog, Humphrey Lhuyd, Rhosier Smyth and John Jones. According to the late Professor G. J. Williams, Roger Morris was 'yr unig gopïwr pwysig yn yr unfed ganrif ar bymtheg a fabwysiadodd orgraff Gruffydd Robert'.[51] Siôn Dafydd Rhys, Henry Salesbury, Henri Perri and Thomas Wiliems all devised various forms in orthography. They were, all of them, as doomed to failure as was Gian Giorgio Trissino's attempt to introduce Greek letters into Italian orthography.[52]

It has been suggested that the orthographic reforms proposed in the sixteenth century were a means of securing unified usage in the vernaculars. To Humphrey Prichard, the glory of language lay in its uniformity.[53] Proper, accepted speech had become the desideratum of the court in Western Europe, and to a certain extent, Welsh humanist scholars viewed their fellow countrymen as potential courtiers. Since, as Gruffydd Robert observed,

Gramadeg yụ celfyḍyd, i ḍoedyd ag i' scrifennu pob ymadroḍ yn goụir, ag yn gyfaḍas.[54]

it is not surprising that as in Italy, France and England, so in Wales, scholars produced grammars to this end. Thus, Gruffydd Robert stated that his grammar contained

ḷauer o bynciau anhepcor i vn a chụennychai na doedyd y gymraeg yn ḍilediaith, nai scrifennu'n iaụn.[55]

The stability which grammar books imposed on language was essential to its proper cultivation,

. . yn fymarni, gorau oeḍ yn gyntaf son am ramadeg: Canys o ḍyno byḍai ḍechrau, os mynnem i'r iaith gynnyḍu yn ḷụydiannus.[56]

He knew the labours of continental scholars and how their analysis of language had brought to light features which had previously remained unnoticed. He condemned the conservative methods of the bards,

> Yr yḍoeḍ y beirḍ rhyd cymru yn ceissio fynghadụ rhag coḷi ne gymyscu a'r saefnaeg. Ond nid oeḍ genthynt phorḍ yn y byd, nag i ḍangos yn fyrr, ag yn hyphord yr odidoụgrụyḍ syḍ ynof rhagor nog meụn laụer o ieithoed, na chụaith i fanegi rhessom am fagod o ḍirgelion a gaid i gụeled, ond chụilio yn fanụl amdanynt, mal y mae gramadegrụyr da yn gụneuthụr, paub in i iaith ihun.[57]

In 1592, Siôn Dafydd Rhys published his INSTITUTIONES, . . certain of the opportuneness of his undertaking,

> . . a' chanbhod o honobh' yr iaith o eisieu Grammâdec Cymráec ynn myned megis arr gybhyrgolh;[58]

He had seen how grammar books had served other languages,

> nyd oes na phordh na môdh 'welh ynn y byd i 'warchâdw iaith rhac ei cholhi, no gwneuthur Grāmâdec idhi ac o honi. Ac ynn y môdh hynny, y cadwyd heb gybhyrgolhi yr Hebráec a''r Gróec, a''r Lhadin, a''r Arabiaith, a''r Caldáec &c.[59]

Humphrey Prichard remarked how the niceties of the language had come to light in the grammar,

> . . olim nubibus velata, nunc autem Cambrobrytannicæ huius Grammaticæ auxilio è tenebris vindicata.[60]

The grammar was regarded as

> gorchwyl mor odidawg . . i dhysgu yr iaith gymraeg:

by Wiliam Midleton in 1593.[61] Salesbury's A BRIEFE AND A PLAYNE INTRODUCTION . . of 1550 contained the first phonetic treatise on Welsh and may therefore be mentioned with the other grammars of the period, Gruffydd Robert's DOSBARTH BYRR. . 1567, Siôn Dafydd Rhys's INSTITUTIONES . . 1592, and Henry Salesbury's GRAMMATICA BRITANNICA, 1593. They all demonstrate a concern for the language and a belief in the importance of grammar to the well-being of the vernacular. But all of them were insufficient and unsatisfactory; Gruffydd Robert lacked the intimate knowledge of Welsh poetry which such a study demanded, and much of Siôn Dafydd Rhys's work was a digest of Latin grammar. Dr. Thomas Parry has referred to ' . . ceisio o'r awdur ystumio a llurgunio'r iaith Gymraeg i ffitio ffrâm gramadeg yr iaith Ladin'.[62] In this he differed little from many of his continental contemporaries. Robert Hall has remarked how, 'Latin grammatical categories were transferred directly to Italian grammar, sometimes most inappropriately, as in Bembo's attempt to assign to the article the function of "segnacaso" or case-sign'.[63]

Not until 1621 did a substantial grammar of Welsh appear; it was the work of Dr. John Davies, ANTIQUAE LINGUAE BRITANNICAE . . , and it was the result of a lifetime of careful study of the language of the poets from Dafydd ap Gwilym to Wiliam Llŷn. Davies referred to his industry,

> Cum igitur in huius linguæ studio vltrà triginta annos, vacantibus horis, sim versatus, quibus vtrique S.S. Bibliorum interpreti Br. indignus fui administer, . .[64]

In 1633, Dafydd Rowland described the author as

> y gwr sanctaidd llên a gorshibiol Doctor Davies, yr hwn a bureiddiodd, a iawn drefnodd ac a berffeiddiodd yr iaith hon, fel i mae i amal lyfrau dysgedig, . . yn ysbusu i ni, . .[65]

It was the crown of humanist achievement in Wales; using the evidence of centuries' old poetic practice, made available by the manuscript collecting and copying of the previous years, he was able to establish the language of the poets as the canon of correct usage. It is significant that the only grammar of any substantial influence appeared at the end of the period of Renaissance and Reformation activity in Wales. In England, Paul Greaves in his GRAMMATICA ANGLICANA commented that the English had become eloquent before they were grammatical. Though, in much of their work, Welsh humanists had inherited the treasures of medieval writers, they were not content to accept the past language merely as it was; their minds were too full of new ideas to do that. It was a period when language was changing rapidly, when there was prolific word-formation and juggling with parts of speech. By 1621, it was time to take stock and to establish a reference work of 'bel usage'.

It was one of the aims of humanism to bring learning to the court of the prince and to refine the art of courtly conversation. As Mr. Saunders Lewis has explained, 'od oedd iaith gwlad i brifio'n iaith pendefigaeth newydd y Dadeni, rhaid oedd iddi ymddieithrio megis Lladin neu Roeg oddi wrth iaith sathredig y bobl gyffredin, a magu urddas geirfa a throeon ymadrodd a dulliau mynegiant ar wahân'.[66]

In Wales, humanism and protestantism became so clearly allied, that writers in the main assumed a didactic responsibility, but that did not prevent their finding in Rhetoric a means of embellishing their native language. Mr. Lewis has referred to Salesbury's figures of speech as an example of such 'ymddieithrio'.[67] This is not wholly correct; his figures were intended ostensibly for the use of the poets. Rhetoric exploited to the full the potentialities of the modern vernaculars and garnished them by

> 'mwrthod a phob ymadrodh anhyodl, symyl, wrth ymarbher ar troelhau, a'r phygurau; y rhei bhal ser, neu bhain gwerthbhawr a 'wnant agwedh pob ymadrodh yn dhisclair.[68]

Salesbury determined to use this means of embellishment for Welsh. In vivid metaphor he affirmed how, by the aid of the figures of speech, he was

> [megis] vn yn translatio nev yn newidio hen vanachloc ahei dortur, hi chapitwl, [hi] chor ahei chapeleu yn neuaddblas, [yn] siambreu, yn estavelli ac yn barlyr[eu], . .[69]

Gruffudd Hiraethog's '[t]raserch ar yr Jaith'[70] had compelled Salesbury to

> estyn hyn yma o ffigurae megis yn golofneu, yn oseilieû, ac attegion ei dodi wrthei.[71]

Henri Perri's work was intended for a wider audience. Henry Salesbury, who himself attempted to prove the vernacular with his GRAMMATICA BRITANNICA, praised Perri for 'trwssio'r iaith' and Lodowicke Lloid claimed,

> He quickened Cambria halfe being dead, and gaue to
> Cambria Marts:
> He shadow'd Greece in Cambria soile, & broght frō
> Greece their Arts . .[72]

To Perri, the devices of Rhetoric were essential in treating the varied subjects which had become the interest of all men during the sixteenth century,

> . . y mae phraethineb yn dyscu phraethebu, ac araitho yn hyodl mywn Duwindeb, medhiginiaeth, cybhreithwriaeth, milwriaeth, ac ym mhob cytro ym mhlith dynion.[73]

The numerous copies of Salesbury's treatise,[74] together with the sections devoted to Rhetoric in the grammar books of Gruffydd Robert,[75] Simwnt Fychan,[76] Wiliam Cynwal,[77] Siôn Dafydd Rhys,[78] Tomas Prys[79] and John Davies,[80] reveal how much

Welsh humanists believed in the study as a means of 'illustrating' the native language.

But apart from making available and even exploiting the existing elements of the vernacular as the works of Grammar and Rhetoric strove to do, there was need for additional embellishment. The Welsh humanists inherited all the methods devised by continental and English scholars: borrowing from classical languages and other modern vernaculars; the extension of meaning of words already in the vocabulary; the improvisation of existing elements in the language, modified by compounding and by the employment of prefix and suffix. In one respect, however, as has already been suggested, they differed from some of their counterparts in Western Europe; there the use of older words of the vocabulary was restricted, in the main, to the realm of poetry, and such words were used with some apprehension in prose works.[81] In Wales, where the belief in the literary achievements of previous centuries was high, this method of enrichment became the chief source, and one of lasting significance, as the subsequent history of the language has revealed.

It was a happy chance for Welsh humanism that it brought with it an antiquarian interest. In Wales, the eyes of scholars were turned not only to the glorious past of Greece and Rome but also to the achievements of the Welsh vernacular in preceding centuries. Such achievements had been best recorded in the work of the poets, the 'vetustæ linguæ custodes';[82] they had preserved unchanged the language of the schools and were the very masters of it,

> yn benseiri yr [Jaith] ac yn enwedic er pan ddarvu am y[r] Araithwyr.[83]

They were the

> scriptionis & pronunciationis, certi, peritissimique magistri, . .[84]

But it was not only the work of the poets which attracted the attention of the humanists; there were the prose-works – religious tracts, lives of saints, romances, histories, grammars and technical treatises of the law, all very well worth recovering from the diaspora created by the dissolution of the monasteries, and by the social reorganization of the times. In them, humanist and reformation scholars saw the opportunity of recreating a language fit for expression in the sixteenth century; in them they saw the possibility of recovering the vernacular from the degraded state into which it had fallen. It was no mere coincidence that many of the scholars who copied and collected manuscripts during the century were also the authors of books of paramount literary influence during the period, and even those who were not immediately associated with the antiquarian movement, indirectly felt its influence.

South Wales appears to have been the home of many of the more important manuscripts in the fifteenth century and the first half of the sixteenth century.[85] Among other important collections were THE BLACK BOOK OF CARMARTHEN, THE BOOK OF TALIESIN, THE BOOK OF ANEIRIN, THE RED BOOK OF HERGEST, THE BOOK OF THE ANCHORITE, and THE WHITE BOOK OF RHYDDERCH. However, most of the important manuscripts, except THE RED BOOK OF HERGEST, THE BOOK OF TALGARTH and THE BOOK OF THE ANCHORITE, were in North Wales by *c.* 1560–1580, and from 1570, they were being copied and studied assiduously by humanists in the Vale of Clwyd. Among them were Humphrey Lhuyd,[86] William Salesbury, Wiliam Midleton, Henri Perri, Thomas Wiliems, David Powell, Henry Salesbury, David Johns, Rhisiart Langford, Roger Morris, John Davies and John Jones. Poets like Simwnt Fychan and Wiliam Cynwal also took part. Earlier, Gruffudd Hiraethog had shown something of the humanist regard for older books and he had tried to appropriate manuscripts for inspection and copying. Salesbury referred to his zeal in 1552,

> . . gan dy welet t[i] Gruffydd, dy hûn mor hiraethoc am gyweir yr Jaith ac ydd wyt (mal y dyw[eit] y llatinveirdd am Atlas) yn kymryt gor[modd] baich ar dy ysgwydd vnigawl, nid am[gen] nath vod yn keisio ymhel o yma ac o yackw am pop hen kwrach o lyfyr brycheulyd ei ddarllen ac ei chwiliaw drostaw, er cahel peth kymporth tuac gynnal yr iaith sydd yn kychwyn ar dramgwydd.[87]

By the second half of the sixteenth century, there were four main groups concerning themselves with the older literature, the bards; the humanists (among them those interested in the old literature as so much historical data, e.g. Humphrey Lhuyd, or as sources of vocabulary, e.g. Thomas Wiliems); the Protestants who sought for confirmation of the early British church, (Dr.

Robin Flower has referred to Bishop Richard Davies and Archbishop Parker, 'seeking in ancient documents evidence making against what the Reformation church held to be the corruptions of Rome'[88]); and those members of the upper classes, e.g. Sir Edward Stradling, whose interest had been motivated by the humanists themselves.

The group in the Vale of Clwyd studied all kinds of earlier Welsh literature which came into their hands, and to many of them, the greatest concern was the language of the older texts. In this, they had inherited the interest of the 'penceirddiaid'. A manuscript in the autograph of John Jones related the three 'cof' which the bards were expected to master,

> And the second of the sayd thre *cof* is the languaige of the Bruttons for which thee Bards ought to giue accompt for every word and sillable therein when they are demaunded thereof and to preserue the auncient tonge & not to intermix ytt wyth any forrayne tonge or to bring any forrayne word amongest yt to the preiudice of there owne words wheareby they might eyther be forgotten or extyrped.[89]

It was this careful concern with language in the earlier poets, together with the purity and copiousness of the language at that period which attracted the attention of the humanist scholars and which demanded of them scrutiny of the older texts. It was their endeavour not only to enhance the prestige of the language by the re-discovery of their own classical literature, but more important, to place at the disposal of the potential writers of Wales, the vocabularies which they not only found in the transcriptions of the works of the earlier bardic teachers, but which they supplemented by their own reading of the earlier literature.

The humanists, however, were not induced to print very much of the old literature but continued in the traditional way to distribute such material and make it available for consultation. One early exception to this was the publication of proverbs, the earliest collection of which was to be found in THE BLACK BOOK OF CHIRK, and other early collections in PENIARTH MS 17, in THE WHITE BOOK OF RHYDDERCH and THE RED BOOK OF HERGEST.[90] During the second half of the sixteenth and the beginning of the seventeenth century, they were collected and classified ready for publication by William Salesbury, Thomas Wiliems and John Davies. There were two main reasons for this activity. One was the impetus given by the popularity of proverbs in England at the time; Salesbury referred to John Heywood, Polydore Vergil and Erasmus;[91] Thomas Wiliems referred to Erasmus.[92] The other was the realization of their value as representing the preserve of the learning and language of the vernacular. Wiliems made his collection so that,

> Yma y galh y cymro glan weled deualh a gwybod, athrylith, diwioldeb, a synwyr natiriol yr hen gymru an henafied ni yn r̂ hen bethau y gallant ymgystadlu ag ûn gyffrediniaith yn Ewropa, o dhyval ystriw ag astud vyvyrdawd . .[93]

It is significant that Salesbury chose a collection of proverbs as his first printed contribution to Welsh literature and scholarship. Apart from inheriting the general interest in proverb collecting which characterized the time, his motives were twofold; to show 'anueidrawl ddoethineb Deo'[94] and to collect words in preparation for his greater work of translating the Gospel.[95] In his preface to OLL SYNNWYR PEN . ., he confessed his debt to Gruffudd Hiraethog whose collection of proverbs he had utilized. Such work was part of the apparatus 'tu ac at perfeithio r iaith',[96] and it was a means of demonstrating

> doethineb yr iaith ne r nasion ae dychymygawdd yn gyntaf.[97]

The antiquity of such words and dialectal differences referred to in his slight apologia to readers,

> . . a bydd vn ddiareb o hanynt mor tywyll (yn aill ai y can heneint yr iaith, ai o ran llediaith y vro, . .)[98]

were in themselves sources of augmenting the tongue. Proverbs were a convenient way of acquainting young writers with 'phrases yr jaith',[99] so Salesbury re-issued his OLL SYNNWYR PEN . . in an enlarged edition in 1567. He felt that such a list might be further supplemented and for that purpose the book was printed,

> bob ailres yn vers ag yn bapyr gwyn, . .[100]

John Davies printed his 'Adagia Britannica' at the end of his dictionary to illustrate the 'sapientiæ reliquias'[101] of the Welsh.

It has been shown that the invention of printing created a desire for uniformity in language, and though the stringency of the bardic tradition had demanded consistent usage among the poets, the widening of the audience and authors of the language in the sixteenth century brought to light certain diversities of practice. Consciousness of dialect differences was expressed during the period,

> Neq equū sit me subiici Demetarū iudicio, quippe qui natione Venetus demetici dialecti imperitus fortasse scripserim non solum aliqua uocabula, uerūetiam sententias (nam utrisq dissidemus) eorū auribus aliquid absurdū, stultū, aut impiū significantes, . .[102]

In 1573, Humphrey Lhuyd surveyed the Welsh dialects,

> [*Ceredigion*] Their tōgue (as Gyraldus affirmeth) is esteemed y[e] finest, of al the other people of wales. And *Gwynedh:* the purer, w[t]out permixtion, cōmyng nearest vnto thauncient British. But the Southerne most rudest, & coursest, bycause it hath greatest affinitie with strange tōgues.[103]

Rhys Amheurug detected certain differences in the speech of those living in Glamorgan,

> Such as remayne at this day of the posterity of the Conquerours (which are but few), inhabite either the Townes, or in the lowe Country neere the Sea Side, who in names and speech differ from the ancient Glamorganians.[104]

Since it became the chief concern of those using the vernacular for purposes of instruction, to reach all people, the language faced the axiomatic demand of being at once national and local. Instead of creating a difficulty as it might have done, it became an acquisition to the tongue. The didactic nature of much of the literature necessitated the use of dialect forms; the author of the DRYCH stated,

> Hynn . . a wnaeth i mi yn y llyfr yma gytgymyscu geiriau r Deheudir a geirieu Gwynedd, pan fyddant heb gytuno, sef i gael o bawb or ddwywlad ddyallt y llyfr yma.[105]

As a result of the dialect commerce of the sixteenth century, many words and meanings, which had hitherto been the preserve of one dialect, became with the printed word, with the consent of Salesbury, Morgan and other writers, a permanent part of the literary language as a whole.

Another means by which the language might be enriched was by the exploitation of existing elements, modifying them by the employment of prefix and suffix, by compounding and by extension of meaning. The derivative method was widely advocated in the sixteenth century; there was nothing new in it, but old prefixes and suffixes which had fallen into disuse were resuscitated and given wider application. The method pleased the purists, who, like Sir John Cheke, conceived the possibility of 'the mould of our own tung' serving 'to fascion a woord of our own'.[106] In Italy, Ercole Strozzi commended the re-introduction of old words to combine to form new ones; in France a volume of 1540 treated of

> Aucunes reigles et observations en general pour scauoir former les verbes, & en especial pour tous motz deriuatifz.[107]

In 1579, Henri Estienne spoke of

> Facilité qu'a le français de former des mots composés, verbes, noms, . .[108]

a capacity which Peter Heylyn claimed to be at its best in English. As late as 1594, however, Nash asserted,

> Our English tongue of all languages most swarmeth with the single money of monosillables, which are the onely scandall of it. Bookes written in them and no other seeme like shop-keepers boxes, that contain nothing else save half-pence, three-farthings and tow-pence. Therefore, what did me I, but having a huge heape of those worthlesse shreds of small English in my *Pia Maters* purse to make the royaller shew with them to mens eyes, had them to the compounders immediately and exchanged them foure into one and others into more, according to the Greek, French, Spanish and Italian.[109]

Welsh certainly had no such 'scandall'. The poets had, over the centuries, exploited to the full the facility which they found the language showed for compounding and for the employment of prefix and suffix. This capacity had been applied recklessly in the 'areithiau'.[110] The humanist scholars in Wales were conversant with such works, and Humphrey Prichard, prefacing the INSTITUTIONES of Siôn Dafydd Rhys, considered it as one of the particular merits of Welsh that it possessed such a capacity for word-formation.

> Cæterùm Cymræorum lingua, compositione non tantùm quatuor, sed & quinque, vel sex, aut forsitan pluribus vocibus, vna eadémque dictione compositâ comprehensis pulcherrimè pollet; veluti,
>
> Cymhletheurgrwydrgeindorch. . .
>
> Vide hæc & plura huiusmodi in Mabinogio & in Historia Gigantum.[111]

No Welsh scholar of the sixteenth century analysed more carefully the nature of word-formation than Gruffydd Robert. He demonstrated the significance of prefixes such as go-, gor-, ḷed-, gụrth-, ad-, dad-, cy-, and among the suffixes which he analysed were -yḍ, -yḍiaeth, -ụr, -ad, -aụdr, -ant, -fa, -aụg, -og, -lon, -ḷon, -ụs, -ig, -ḷyd, -gar. To the humanist scholars, compounding was no mere process of joining words together in a haphazard fashion; there was science in their methods, and respect for previous practice in the language. Gruffydd Robert enumerated the systems of combination available to the Welsh author,

> Mo. Pessaụl ansaụd syḍ i henụ? Gr. tair. s. ansaụḍ sengl, ansaụḍ gyfansoḍedig, ag ail gyfansoḍedig. O'r sengl ansaụd y byḍ gair pryd na ụneler ef o gyssụḷt amryụ eiriau, mal: duụ, . . o'r ail ansaụḍ y byḍ, pan ụneler gair o gyssụlt dau amrafaeḷ eiriau, mal: geuduụ, . . O'r drydeḍ ansaụḍ y byḍ gair, pan ụneler ef o gyssụlt tri gair ynghyd, mal: anghyfiaith, . .[112]

The variety of forms like *adgodiad*, *adgyfodiat*, *ailgyfodedigaeth*, *ailgyfodiad*, *cyfodedigaeth*, *cyfodiad*, *cyfodiadigeth*, all found in use during the period to express the same idea shows that the semantic signification of prefixes and suffixes was still fluid; and as is true of so many English forms coined at the same time, it is often difficult to understand why some remained and why others disappeared permanently from the vocabulary.

The inadequacy of language caused by the influx of new ideas had found expression earlier. The translator of the TRACTATUS DE ARMIS not only recognized a dearth of significants to express technical terminology, but also suggested a remedy,

> . . am vod iaith Gymraec mor anaml na cheffir ohoni ddigon o eirieu perthynol i'r gwaith newydd hwnn, rraid yw ymwest ar ieithiau eraill lle bo hi diffygiol, megys ydd ym mewn petheu eraill, ac y mae pob iaith ar i gilydd.[113]

In the sixteenth century, there were new ideas which demanded new words; there were old ideas which, in the ferment of the age, had acquired new and specialized meanings. Frequently, in both cases, it seemed to be easier and more expedient to borrow, not only the ideas, but also the significants to express such ideas.

Though Greek, which had been in abeyance for much of the

Middle Ages, was now included in the university curriculum, it never challenged the prestige of Latin in the minds of the humanists. But borrowing from Latin did not merely mean adopting words from that tongue into Welsh; they had to be naturalized to take their place properly in the fabric of the language, as Gruffydd Robert realized,

> rhaid edrych yn graph, & chadụ yn ḍyfal y moḍ syḍ iụ gụneuthur nhụy yn camreig. ag megis pann el un o'r naiḷ grefyḍ i'r ḷaḷ, ef a neụidia i gụcụḷ ai ụisc felly ụrth ḍụyn gair o'r iaith bigiliḍ, e neụidia i derfyn, ag ụeithiau lythrennau eraiḷ, a mụy yn y gamraeg nog meụn iaith yn y byd.[114]

Other languages, too, considered such adaptation necessary. In 1516, Francesco Fortunio referred to

> la mutazione delle vocali [e delle consonanti] nelle volgari voci del latino discendenti.[115]

and Claudio Tolomei in his CESANO examined the changes of words like 'plenus', 'clavis', '[af]latus' into 'pieno', 'chiave' and 'fiato',[116] In France, Robert Estienne discussed

> De Permvtatione Literarum in vocabulis Latinis quum fiunt Gallica.[117]

The first to analyse the Latin element in Welsh was William Salesbury; in 1547, in the introduction to his dictionary he stated,

> Geirieu llatin a ledieithant ir saesonaec neu ir Camberaec a newidiant x / am s / val y geirieu hyn / *crux* crosse croes ne crws / *exemplum* esampyl / *extendo* estennaf: *excomunicatus* escomyn.

These rudiments were enlarged in his A BRIEFE AND A PLAYNE INTRODUCTION . . of 1550, and further augmented in 1567 when he discussed the development of Latin 'v',

> Also *g* is added to the beginning of such words as be deriued of the Latine, whych begyn with *v*, as *Gvvilim*, *gvvic*, *gvvynt*, *Gvvent*, *gvvin*, *gosper*, of *VVilielmus*, *vicus*, *ventus*, *Venta*, vinum, vesper.[118]

A note in HAVOD MANUSCRIPT 26 illustrates two methods by which Welshmen sought to increase the vocabulary; borrowing from Latin (governed by phonetic rules) and the further employment of prefix and suffix to such borrowed words,

> Tymp a drychir o Tempus amser, . . Ac or tymp y daw,

> tymphic vn a aner yn ei amser, ac anhymic Abortiuus, vn a aner allan oi amser. Ac or genedio Temporis y daw tymmor, amser, tymmoraidd amserawl, peth a wneler yn ei amser, neû a vo parod oi gymerûd yn ei amser. . .[119]

The fullest treatment of the Latin element came in Gruffydd Robert's grammar; he compiled the section devoted to it in order to

> . . dangos phorḍ deg, a gụedaiḍ i ụneuthur gair ḷadin yn gamraegaiḍ pan fo eissio gair camraeg cyfattebaụl, i'r ḷadin, ne i'r groeg ag edrych pa foḍ y ḷuniai 'r cymru gynt y cyfryụ eiriau.[120]

Among his examples illustrating phonetic development are old established words in the vocabulary side by side with his own coinings used by him and by Rhosier Smyth,

> . . P, yn y cyfryụ loeḍ a dry yn ,b, ,d, yn ḍ, cupidus cybyḍ ,t, yn ,d, mal uitrum gụydr, . . c yn, g, consecro cyssegru. g, a daụḍ Aegiptus Eipht, . . tromlefn ar ol ,r, a dry iụ chrech anianaụl. porta porth, . . ,ct, yn th, perfectus perfaith, . . ,cc, yn ,ch, siccus sych, . . da hefyd oeḍ farcio pa derfyn a roḍer i'r gair, mal uictima, gụithifen, . . absoluo, absolfen . .[121]

Wales was later than other European countries in using the printing press, and so many languages were already 'vrddedic o bob rhyw oreuddysc', as Salesbury remarked of English in 1547.[122] It is natural, then, that Gruffydd Robert, abroad in Milan, witnessing how other countries had partaken of such '[g]oreuddysc', should recommend borrowing from modern languages as a secondary source of enrichment. He expounded his doctrine concerning neologizing

> . . y neb a chụennycho fod yn hyodl, . . yn y gamraeg rhaid iḍo edrych yn gyntaf dim, a oes un gair arferedig ymlhith y cymru eussus, i yspressu i feḍụl, . . Onid oes; rhaid benthygio yn gyntaf gen y ḷadin, os geḷḷir yn ḍiụrthnyssig i gụneuthur yn gymreigaiḍ: os byḍ caledi yma, rhaid ḍụyn i nechụyn, gan yr eidalụyr, phrancod, ysphaenụyr, ag od oes geiriau saesneg ụedi i breinio ynghymru ni ụasnaetha moi gụrthod nhụy.[123]

As a result of such borrowing, he maintained that Welsh could compare with other modern languages in dealing with the new subjects of the sixteenth century,

> Canys ụrth y cydnabod a gefais ag ieithoeḍ erail̦, yn hụyr yroụron mi a'l̦af pan fynnụyf gael genthynt bob peth a berthyn at gampau, a chynnedfau gụyr rhinụeḍol, gynghordioleḍ gamradeg, flodeuau retorigyḍiæth, ystriụ dialectigyḍiæth, coụreinrhụyd meḍygon, pụyl̦eḍ dinassụyr, gụybodaeth philosophyḍion, gorchestion milụyr, dụụioldeb theologyḍiæth . .[124]

Neologisms called for justification. In England, Richard Eden declared,

> I Dare saye without arrogancie, that to translate the variable historie of Plinie into our toonge, I wolde be ashamed to borowe so muche of the Latine as he Doth of the Greke, althowgh the Latine toonge be accompted ryche, and the Englysshe indigent and barbarous,[125]

The same defence of borrowing was preferred in Welsh. Gruffydd Robert explained how first Latin had borrowed from Greek, and other modern languages had enriched themselves from Latin,

> mi a ụclaf y l̦adinụyr oeḍ gyụaethog i hiaith, yn benthygio gen y groegụyr laụer gair, yn y cyfryụ leoeḍ, y Phrancod, yspaenụyr a'r Eidalụyr, yn ḍiḍeincod yn cymryd i nechụyn gen y l̦adin. a'r hen gymru gynt ụedi tynnu yrhann fụyaf o'r geiriau al̦l̦an o'r l̦adin, ne'r groeg, ni ḍylai fod arnominnau mor cyụiliḍ ụrth fenthygio i helaethu'r iaith, gen y neb a roes inni i dechreuad . .[126]

Rhosier Smyth, disciple of Gruffydd Robert in matters of language, repeated part of this justification in 1611,

> Yn ḍiụaethaf na ryfeḍa fymod ryụ Amser yn benthygio gairiau (pen fytho eisiau) gen y l̦aḍin. canys yr hen gymru oeḍynt yn arfer yrun peth, megis ygel̦ir gueled yn haụḍ, ḍarfod tynu 'rhan fụya o'n iaith ni al̦au o'r ladin, yr hụn beth y mae'r Athraụ uchod yn i ḍangos yn i lyfr o gyfiachydiaeth, . .[127]

Morris Kyffin borrowed with the 'bashfulnes' that characterized Sir John Cheke's neologizing.[128] Necessity, not eloquence was Kyffin's reason for borrowing, and he found justification for it in the practice of other languages,

> Eithr am ryw air angenrheidiol, yr hwn ni ellid dangos mo sylwedd ei rym, na synnwyr ei arwyddoccâd yn gymraeg, e ddarfu i mi yn-ôl arfer yr iaith *Saesonaeg*, *Ffrangaeg*,

> iaith *Itali*, iaith *Spaen*, a bagad o ieithoedd eraill, gymryd y cyfryw air o'r *Groeg*, neu o'r *Lladin*, yn y modd y mae'n gynefin gan-mwyaf ymhôb gwlad yngHred er ys-talm o amser. Nid oes nēmawr o'r fath eiriau;[129]

Kyffin anticipated criticism of his neologisms,

> mi a wna gyfri gael fy-marnu a beio arnaf gan ryw fath a'r goeg ddynion, y rhai a graffant ar ymbell air, ymma ag accw, ag a ddoedant yn y fan, wele, geiriau seisnigaidd a geiriau lladingaidd yw rhain, yn dwyno 'r gymraec:[130]

To such criticism, his reply was twofold; of Latin words,

> pwy nis gwyr nad yw'r iaith Gymraec yn ei herwydd, ddim amgen, onid hanner lladin drwyddi.[131]

Of words from the modern vernaculars,

> Mi' allwn pe bae gennyf hamdden wneuthyr llyfr digon ei faint o'r geirieu cymreic arferedig, a fenthycciwyd nid yn vnig o'r *Lladin* a'r *Ffrangaec*, eithr o *iaith Itali*, ag *iaith Spaen* hefyd: heblaw'r *dafod Roeg*, ag *Ebryw*, a'r cyfryw.[132]

Once the printing of books had established a generally accepted vocabulary, writers sought justification for neologisms on the pretext of their having been used previously. Rhosier Smyth found consent in the work of the 'Athrau'; similarly, when Huw Lewys used the word 'perl', he appended an explanation,

> na fid rhyfedd, na chwith genyt, paham yr henwais y llyfr hwn yn berl, (gann mae gair Saesonaeg yw perl) nid wyf yn gwneuthyr yn hynn ond fal y gwnaeth fyngwell om blaen, canys darllain y trydydd pennod ar ddeg o Efangyl Sainct Mathew, yn y 45. ar chweched wers a deugain, a thi a gai yr vn gair.[133]

Many who criticized the ink-horn elements in the translation of Scripture into English, criticized them because they defeated the purpose of being intelligible to the people at large. There were those writers in Welsh who realized the difficulties of going to the older sources to furnish vocabulary for religious works. Though Kyffin's condemnation of Salesbury's translation was directed more at the Latinizations than at the antiquity of the vocabulary,

> E ddarfuessid cyfieuthu'r Testament newydd ynghylch yr wythfed neu'r nowfed flwyddyn o Deyrnas eyn harglwyddes frenhines *Elizabeth*, ond yr oedd cyfled llediaith a chymaint anghyfiaith yn yr ymadrodd brintiedig, na alle clust gwir

> Gymro ddioddef clywed mo 'naw'n iawn.[134]

yet there was censure also for Salesbury's archaisms which was both expressed and defended by Thomas Wiliems,

> A chyd bair andyscedic yn beiaw ar ei ymchweliad ir Camberaec (o bleit buan y barn pob ehud) eto y neb a ddarlleno Cronic y Brutanieid a'r tywysogion, Cyfrai[th] hoell dda ap Cadell, cywyddae a cherddae prydyddion celfydd yn yr iaith y Cyfraith Camberaec a welawdd ef, ac amryw o hen lyvrae, Siarterae ac eraill o hen goffae . .[135]

Many, however, refused such a means of enriching the language. The author of the DRYCH explained,

> pe i bysswn i yn dethol allan hen eirieu Cymraeg nyd ydynt arferedig, ny byssei vn ym mysc cant yn dyall hanner a ddywedasswn, cyd byssei yn Gymraeg da: am fod yr iaith gyphredin wedy ei chymyscu a llawer o eirieu anghyfieith sathredig ymhlith y bobl, a bod yr hen eirieu a r wir Gymraeg wedy myned ar gyfyrgoll a i habergofi. Amherthynas wrth hynn a fuassei ymarfer o araith heb nemor yn ei ddeallt.[136]

where language for popular instruction took precedence as it did a century later in ALLWYDD PARADWYS,

> . . oblegid nid fy mryd i yw dysgu yr iaith, . . ond fy amcan yn unic yw, ennynnu o'r Devotionau hyn Dduwioldeb yn eich calonnau chwi.[137]

Such didactic writers professed preference for the common usage, for as Caxton observed in 1490,

> comyn termes that be dayli vsed ben lyghter to be vnderstonde then the olde and auncyent englysshe.[138]

Richard Owen apologized for the inferiority of his Welsh, but added,

> mi ai rrois mal i gellir i ddallt yn sathredic . .[139]

Such intelligibility was of primary importance in religious works; the Preface to the Authorized Version of the English Bible in 1611 stated,

> But we desire that the Scripture may speake like it selfe, as in the language of Canaan, that it may bee vnderstood euen of the very vulgar.[140]

In the same way, the author of the DRYCH affirmed,

> Canys fynghyngyd am meddwl yn bennaf yn y llyfr hynn yw rhoi cynghor sprydol ir annysgedig. Ag er mwyn cael gan y cyphredin ddeall y llyfr er daioni iddynt, mi a ddodais

> fy meddwl i lawr a cheir eu bronneu hwy yn yr iaith gyphredinaf a sathrediccaf ymhlith y Cymry yrowron.[141]

Morris Kyffin made a similar statement in 1595,

> Mi a dybiais yn oref adel heibio'r hen eiriau cymreig yr rhai ydynt wedi tyfu allan o gydnabod a chyd-arfer y cyffredin, ag a ddewisais y geiriau howssaf, rhwyddaf, a sathredicca 'g allwn, i wneuthyr ffordd yr ymadrodd yn rhydd ag yn ddirwystrus i'r sawl ni wyddant ond y gymraeg arferedig.[142]

This was part of Kyffin's language 'credo', for he had expressed the same opinion in 1588, in almost identical words, in the preface to his translation into English of Terence's ANDRIA,

> I have used (as neere as I could) the most knowen, vsuall, and familiar phrases in common speech, to expresse the authors meaning . .[143]

The difficulty of new-borrowed terms, either from the older vocabulary or from classical and modern languages, or of new coinages, was met in several ways, many of them common to English neologizers of the period. Some words would become intelligible with usage; Thomas Lupset spoke of the word 'charitie' in 1533,

> And though now at fyrst heryng, this word stondethe straungelye with you, yet by vse it shall waxe familiar, specially when you haue it in this maner expressed vnto you.[144]

Richard Davies referred to the word 'Testament',

> A' thrwy Dduw ny bydd ny-mawr o vlynyddeu nes eto myned y gair Testament yn ddigon sathredic, cyffredin, Cymroaidd, ac yn gwbl ddyallus ei iawn arwyddocaat.[145]

William Salesbury and his co-translators glossed difficult words or dialect usages in the text with marginalia, a method which was explained from the title-page,

> Eb law hyny y mae pop gair a dybiwyt y vot yn andeallus, ai o ran llediaith y 'wlat, ai o ancynefinder y devnydd, wedy ei noti ai eglurhau ar 'ledemyl y tudalen gydrychiol . .[146]

The Catholic translation of the Old Testament into English adopted a similar procedure,

> . . we commonly put the explication in the margent.[147]

Others, such as Elyot in England, proposed to explain words as they were introduced; he maintained that in THE GOVERNOUR,

> there was no terme new made by me of a latine or frenche worde, but it is there declared so playnly by one mene or other to a diligent reder that no sentence is therby made derke or harde to be understande.[148]

For example, when he used 'animate', he appended 'or give courage'. Morris Kyffin also used this method; this explains, in part, why there are so many synonymical pairs in his writing. Morys Clynnog listed difficult words as an appendix to his ATHRAVAETH in 1568; Henri Perri gave classical equivalents for his technical terms of Rhetoric at the end of his treatise; Morris Kyffin explained of his neologisms,

> o'r rhai rheitiaf di a gei hysbysrwydd a deonglad ar eu penneu eu hun, ar ôl diwedd hyn o Rag-ddoediad.[149]

and such words, he listed under the heading,

> Dealld ag arwyddocaad y geiriau angenrheidiol, a dwyswyd i'r Gymraec, yn hyn o lyfr . . PALLIA, Pallau; sef, Mantellau, tebig i'r fâth y mae marchogion y Gardes arfer o'u gwisco. Gwisc lâes arferedig gynt ymhlith Philosophyddion: côp, neu fâth ar simmwr.[150]

But the increasing number of words which were either appearing for the first time or making a reappearance in the Welsh vocabulary in the sixteenth century was more than could be dealt with adequately by means of these temporary measures; scholars found that the only effective way of meeting the problem was by the compilation of dictionaries. The appearance of the dictionaries of Elyot, Cooper and Thomas in England only served to emphasize their importance. As will be shown later, Thomas Thomas's DICTIONARIUM LINGUAE LATINAE ET ANGLICANAE became more than an inspiration to one of the Welsh humanists; for Thomas Wiliems it became the basis of his own TRYSAWR . . . He wished to see a standard dictionary in Welsh,

> val y mae 'mhob gwlat yn y Ghristnocaeth gan mwyaf gan bob cenetlaeth yn eu hieithieu 'hunein, yn gyssylhtedic a'r Lhatin, . .[151]

There were, however, various reasons for the emergence of dictionaries in Wales. Salesbury asserted that he had

> writtē a lytle englyshe dyctionary

in order that Welshmen might

> spedely obteyne the knolege of the englishe tōge.[152]

If that was his aim, the book may be compared with John Palsgrave's LESCLARCISSEMENT DE LA LANGUE FRANCOYSE, 1530, Claudius Holyband's A DICTIONARIE FRENCH AND ENGLISH, 1593, and Richard Percyvall's BIBLIOTHECA HISPANICA, 1591, which was augmented by Minsheu in 1599. To some, a dictionary preserved the intrinsic potentialities of the language and made them available to writers at their pleasure. Conversely, it was a reference book for those who found words borrowed from the older periods of the language difficult to understand, because

> bod yr hen eirieu a r wir Gymraeg wedy myned ar gyfyrgoll a i habergofi.[153]

Since it was an integral part of the Renaissance spirit in Wales to reflect on the past achievements of native literature, the dictionary was a necessary companion to the full understanding of such literature. The compiler of the vocabulary found in PENIARTH MANUSCRIPT 155 (1561–2), remarked,

> Darllain heb ddeall overedd yw ac velly yn gymaint a bod geiriav o hen gymraec yn y llyfr hwnn arveredic gynt ac ni wys beth ynt yn gyffredinol yn y to heddyw ac am hynny er hawshav deall y darlleydd J dodais i hyd J doeth im kof bob gair o hen gymbraec ar sydd yn y llyfr hwn ar ol ordyr yr egwyddor . .[154]

and similarly, in LLANSTEPHAN MANUSCRIPT 86 there is a list of

> Geiriau or hen Gamberaag anhawdh ei dirnad yn yr oes hon,[155]

to which are appended illustrations from the works of the poets. Henry Cockeram's ENGLISH DICTIONARIE of 1623 was compiled,

> to the understanding of the more difficult authors already printed in our Language.[156]

It was also the function of a dictionary to record new words and to grant them official consent in the language, establishing for them an exact area of meaning. Apart from all these considerations, a dictionary was the sure way of demonstrating the copiousness of the language, and as Cockeram said of his work, it led to a

> more speedy attaining of an elegant perfection of the . . tongue. both in reading, speaking and writing.[157]

There was a long tradition of vocabulary making in Wales; it had been an integral part of bardic training over the centuries. Lists of words and synonyms found in the manuscripts constitute part of the preparation which prospective poets were expected to master and commit to memory. The section in the grammars devoted to 'amlder Cymraeg' would infer such a preoccupation with words. To the uninitiate, many of the works of the bards remained unintelligible because they contained words which had either never become part of the spoken language or had disappeared from it. PENIARTH MANUSCRIPT 50 (1415–1456), contains 'a Vocabulary of some of old Welsh words with their modern equivalents',

> Henweu kystedlydd ynt: kyhaual. kychwior. kyfeissior. kyfefell . .[158]

A similar list is found in PENIARTH MANUSCRIPT 27 (*ii*),[159] possibly in the autograph of Gutun Owain. When THE BOOK OF ANEIRIN came into Gwilym Tew's possession, he listed words from the poem, which are preserved in PENIARTH MANUSCRIPT 51,

> Llyma hen gymraec
> :
> Ethi = ysspartvnev
> :
> Trylaw = daear
> Trylen = kad . .[160]

The study continued and PENIARTH MANUSCRIPT 55 which belongs to the end of the century, reveals the same interest in the old vocabulary,

> . . llerw yw arafeiddrwydd . . Awl yw gweddi . . tydwedd yw dayar . . ffaclawr yw ryfelwr . . ffelaic yw arglwydd . . keimiad yw gwgwas dewr . .[161]

Such a tradition persisted into the sixteenth century, and PENIARTH MANUSCRIPT 189, in the autograph of Simwnt Fychan, illustrates how the interest in the bardic vocabulary remained; he listed words in groups according to their initial letters,

> Argledrad = Arglwydd
> Aeserw = tec
> Addien = tec . .[162]

The humanist scholars of the sixteenth century inherited this concern for vocabulary, and one, who, in some ways, belonged to both the old and new tradition, Gruffudd Hiraethog, set about to convert many of the available bardic vocabularies into an alphabetical thesaurus which is preserved in PENIARTH MANUSCRIPT 230; in it he appended to his words, illustrations from the poets,

> Abid abadwisc wynebvs yn i abid Tvdvr Aled
> Aban Ryvel aban a ddaw bevnydd yn in bro ni a bair newyn . . Jolo[163]

Other Renaissance scholars in their manuscript reading, encountered such vocabularies and extracted words from them, or supplemented such lists with further examples. William Salesbury was one of the first to do this; his dictionary of 1547 was not his only lexicographical work; pages 1 to 235 of HAVOD MANUSCRIPT 26, contain a vocabulary alphabetically arranged, illustrated by quotations from the poets, and the epilogue is indicative of the way humanist scholars worked,

> Ac val hynn y tervyna hyn o Athrolythr William Lleyn, gwedy angwanegû o eiriæ lawer a chorectiat Mr Wiliam Salesbury A thalm nid bychan a gesgleis innau 1574: 17 february Liûer Thos Wiliems offeirat.[164]

Salesbury's dictionary of 1547 had been compiled,

> for the vse and behoue of my contry men, ye Walshmen, . .[165]

It was followed by several manuscript vocabularies during the century for the benefit of those who wished to compose in Welsh and understand the older literature. They were drawn up by such men as Roger Morris,[166] Rhisiart Langford, John Jones, Siôn Dafydd Rhys, Thomas Wiliems and John Davies.

In 1607, Thomas Wiliems completed his monumental work, TRYSAWR YR IAITH LATIN AR GYMRAEC, NE'R GEIRIADUR CYWOETHOCAF A HELAETHAF OR WIR DHILETIAITH VRYTANAEC. The pattern was derived largely from the DICTIONARIUM LINGUAE LATINAE ET ANGLICANAE of Thomas Thomas, first printer to the University of Cambridge. That work was, to some extent, an abridgement of Cooper's THESAURUS . . which, in turn, was indebted to Elyot's work. Wiliems's pattern was significant; Welsh was now no longer the language preserved by the poets with a range circumscribed by the limits of their muse and vision. It was about to graft into its being that amount of classical thought which was enshrined in one of the most popular Latin-English lexicons of the day. The late Professor G. J. Williams has compared his methods of enriching the mother-tongue with those of Gruffydd Robert, ' . .nid dangos i lenorion Cymraeg sut i lunio geiriau newydd, eithr cyfoethogi eu geirfa wrth roddi at eu gwasanaeth gasgliad o eiriau wedi eu tynnu o'r hen destunau rhyddiaith, o weithiau'r beirdd ac o'r iaith fyw'.[167]

He *did* coin new words to translate concepts which were being given names for the first time in Welsh, but his main source was the material he found in the old manuscripts. PENIARTH MANUSCRIPT 188, his common-place book finds Wiliems in action, preparing for his great work; it contains vocabularies, glosses and several quotations from poetry, from the laws and from the prose Romances.[168] In the preface to his dictionary, he referred to his work of preparation,

> a daruod y mi er ys mwy na deg mlynedh ar hugein, ag yn wastatol er hyny hyd yr awr honn, bentyrru Casglfa dhiruawr o eiriae Cymraec, henion a newydhion, er mwyn cymoni a chyfansodhi Dictionarium a Geiriadur Brytanaec . .[169]

Bullokar spoke of similar industry in 1616,

> Yet this I will say . . that in my younger yeares it hath cost mee some observation, reading, study and charge: which you may easily beleeve, considering the great store of strange words, our speech doth borrow, not only from the Latine, and Greeke, (and from the ancient Hebrew) but also from forraine vulgar languages round about us: beside sundry olde words now growne out of use, and divers termes of art, . .[170]

Wiliems had included all such words. His remarks on the value of his work are significant. He felt that a dictionary was essential to establish the tongue,

> y gadw'r iaith einom, . . yn dragyvyth, er dig a mefl i Sudhas a holh elynion y loewiaith Vrytanaec;[171]

He also felt that the work might induce respect for the language,

> . . ar hyder y mawrha'n Cymru ni eu priawt ymadrodh a'u cyseuiniaith loewdec, eglurloew'n welh o hynn alhan, . .[172]

The dictionary was to be the power-house of the vernacular,

> Yma gan hyny y ceiph yr hygar a'r mwynlan dharlleydh amlder tramawr ag amryw niueroedh o eiriae detholedic, yn gystal o'r hen Vrutaniaith gynt ag o'r gyphredinaith arueredic yn yr oes honn, hyt y gelhyt haeachen drwy holh Gymru, nyt heb awdurdawt hen a newydh y wirio ag y gadarnhau pob gair anarueredic y pryt hynn, . .[173]

The purpose of including such old words was to promote the study of earlier Welsh literature and history,

> Nys galhwn hepcor heniaith y Brytanieit o'r cynvyt o

> herwydh ei bod yn dra angenrheitiol er mwyn deualhu'r hen Lyurae Chronic ag ereilh hen awdurieit, . .[174]

Both old and new words would equip men to meet the demands imposed on language in the sixteenth century,

> . . nyd yw'n anwybot y neb a synhwyr yn ei benn mor anhepcor, mor gyfreidiol a gwerthuawr yw'r swlht a'r anwyldlws yma, nys gelhir ei gyngwerthydhio, y'r trebelyt areithwyr, y'r precethwyr huawdlion, ag y gyfieithwyr tradoethion pob celuydhyt arbenic o'r gywoethoc Latiniaith y'r geindec Gymraec einom.[175]

This was followed in 1632 by Dr. John Davies's DICTIONARIUM DUPLEX, the first part of which was begun in 1593; the second part, compiled at the request of Sir John Wynn, was a shortened version of Thomas Wiliems's THESAURUS. At the end of his introduction to ANTIQUAE LINGUAE BRITANNICAE . . RVDIMENTA, 1621, he remarked how for thirty years he had studied the Welsh tongue, and the dictionary reflected the same industry. He had read manuscripts and copied many of them. PENIARTH MANUSCRIPT 110, a collection of the poetry of Tudur Aled and others, shows how he noted quotations which he was to use later in his DICTIONARIUM. He copied the poetry of the Gogynfeirdd, he modernized the greater part of THE BLACK BOOK OF CARMARTHEN, he compiled collections of the poetry of Dafydd ap Gwilym and poetry of the sixteenth century; he made a copy of GWASANAETH MAIR – to mention only a selection of his work.[176] A letter from him to Owen Wyn in 1639, acknowledging the loan of four Welsh manuscripts, illustrates what his methods had been,

> . . I have looked upon every particular that is in them, & finde nothing in them but what I have allreadie except some fewe things of the doing of our later prydyddion wch be not much usefull for my purpose. Yet I doe verie earnestlie desier the sight of the rest that yo^u^ write are promised yo^u^. There may be perhaps in the meanest of them some things that I would gladly see.[177]

His reading was wide, though as he explained in the preface to the DICTIONARIUM, there were times when he was uncertain of the meaning of words and would have valued the opinion of other men. Such circumspection prevented his falling into so many of the errors which marred Gwilym Tew's compilation in PENIARTH MANUSCRIPT 51; but times had changed, and scholarship had witnessed a heyday in Wales. Davies's help in the editions of the Bible of 1620 and the Prayer Book of 1621, meant that the matured language of the Renaissance and Reformation was his, too; he utilized it to the full in his dictionary of 1632. The work of Dr. John Davies was the supreme achievement of humanism in Wales.

The Welsh language had been enriched over the years by the employment of prefix and suffix, by compounding, by extension of meaning and by liberal borrowing from the classical and modern languages. But its main source of augmentation had been the recovery of the vocabulary of the poets, and that, exploited. The compiler of ATHENAE OXONIENSES remarked of John Davies that he was,

> esteemed by the academians well vers'd in the history and antiquities of his own nation, and in the Greek and Hebrew languages, a most exact critic, an indefatigable researcher into antient scripts, and well acquainted with curious and rare authors.[178]

Such a description suited more than one of the Renaissance scholars in Wales. It was this research into 'antient scripts' which had been the backbone of language enrichment throughout the century; it saved Welsh from becoming mere 'écumeurs de latin', which earned, in France, Geoffroy Tory's derision in his CHAMPFLEURY of 1529; it saved it from degrading into a mere 'patois' of 'pryny a gwerthy a bwyta ac yfed' which it might well have become had the Welsh Bible and Welsh authors followed the tradition and resources of Elis Gruffudd rather than the riches of the native literary heritage which humanism and protestantism in Wales exploited to the full.

NOTES

1 Havod MS. 26, p. 204. Quoted in *The Bulletin of the Board of Celtic Studies* IX, p. 109.

2 See Ieuan M. Williams, 'Ysgolheictod Hanesyddol yr Unfed Ganrif ar Bymtheg', *Llên Cymru* II, 2, pp.111 ff.

3 Quoted in Glanmor Williams, *Welsh Reformation Essays*, p. 67.

4 Glanmor Williams, *Bywyd ac Amserau'r Esgob Richard Davies*, p. 19.

5 See G. J. Williams, *Gramadeg Cymraeg gan Gruffydd Robert*, pp. xxiii ff.

6 *The Dictionary of Welsh Biography*, pp. 845–846.

7 Ibid., p. 538.

8 *Renaissance Literary Theory and Practice*, p. 5.

9 Gladys Doidge Willcock, Alice Walker (editors), *The Arte of English Poesie*, by George Puttenham. Introduction, p. lxxxv.

10. Quoted in Vernon Hall, *Renaissance Literary Criticism*, p. 23.

11 Morris Kyffin, *Deffynniad Ffydd Eglwys Loegr*, edited by Wm. Prichard Williams, p. [ix].

12 Quoted in J. L. Moore, *Tudor-Stuart Views on the Growth, Status, and Destiny of the English Language*, p. 7.

13 *Gramadeg Cymraeg gan Gruffydd Robert*, edited by G. J. Williams, 'Yr Iaith Gymraeg yn erchi . . '.

14 *Gramadeg Cymraeg.*

15 Quoted in Vernon Hall, p. 98.

16 Ibid., p. 35.

17 Quoted in Robert A. Hall, Jr. *The Italian Questione della Lingua*, Ch.I.

18 *Kynniver llith a ban*, edited by John Fisher. Dedicatory letter.

19 *Antiquae Linguae Britannicae . . Rudimenta*, p. 81.

20 Ibid., p. 85.

21 Quintilian. Quoted in D. L. Clark, *Rhetoric and Poetry in the Renaissance*, p. 24.

22 *Eglvryn Phraethineb*, edited by G. J. Williams, 'Lhythvr Annerch.'

23 Quoted in Vernon Hall, p. 35.

24 A. Ewert, *The French Language*, pp. 11 ff.

25 *The Triumph of the English Language*, p. 139, "The nationalistic spirit . . is so limited in its influence as not to merit much attention".

26 Quoted in Vernon Hall, p. 87.

27 Ibid., p. 90.

28 *Gramadeg Cymraeg*, 'Iaith Gambr yn annerch . . '.

29 Quoted in Vernon Hall, p. 89.

30 Ibid., p. 84.

31 Ibid.

32 Ibid., p. 85.

33 Ibid., p. 87.

34 Ibid., p. 88.

35 Quoted in Richard Foster Jones, *The Triumph of the English Language*, p. 103.

36 Quoted in Vernon Hall, p. 94.

37 Ibid.

38 Havod MS. 26, p. 204.

39 Quoted in Vernon Hall, p. 98.

40 *Critical Prefaces of the French Renaissance*, p. 12.

41 Quoted in Vernon Hall, p. 94.

42 cf. De Witt T. Starnes, Gertrude E. Noyes, *The English Dictionary from Cawdrey to Johnson*, p. 5, "Though Caxton, as a good business man, undoubtedly sought to earn a livelihood from the printing press, he was no less concerned to improve knowledge and raise the level of culture among his countrymen".

43 Quoted in R. Geraint Gruffydd, *Religious Prose in Welsh from the Beginning of the Reign of Elizabeth to the Restoration*, Chapter II, section 2.

44 Quoted in Vernon Hall, p. 98.

45 cf. Richard Foster Jones, p. 47, "So closely was knowledge associated with the classics that any separation of the two was viewed by the educated as a distinct injury to learning".

46 Quoted in Richard Foster Jones, p. 47.

47 Quoted in Louis B. Wright, *Middle-Class Culture in Elizabethan England*, p. 343.

48 Quoted in Richard Foster Jones, p.34.

49 Ibid., p. 35.

50 'Rhagymadrodd Thomas Wiliems i'w Eiriadur', quoted in *Rhyddiaith Gymraeg, Y gyfrol gyntaf*, p. 138.

51 Quoted in Richard Foster Jones, p. 14.

52 Ibid., p. 32.

53 Quoted in Albert C. Baugh, *A History of the English Language*, p. 253.

54 *Yny lhyvyr hwnn*, 'Annerch at y darlheawdyr'.

55 Quoted in Richard Foster Jones, p. 33.

56 Ibid., p. 37.

57 Ibid., p. 44.

58 Ibid., pp. 44–45.

59 Ibid., p. 42.

60 Ibid., p. 126.

61 Ibid., p. 5.

62 Ibid., p. 10.

63 Ibid.

64 Ibid., p.26.

65 Ibid., p. 84.

66 Richard Sherry, *A treatise of Schemes and Tropes*, 'The Epystle'.

67 Gladys Doidge Willcock, Alice Walker, Introduction, p. lxxxv.

68 Quoted in Richard Foster Jones, p. 70.

69 Ibid.

70 Ibid., p. 73.

71 Ibid.

72 *English Poetry and the English Language*, pp. 34–35.

73 Richard Foster Jones, p. 211.

74 *Poetic Diction in the English Renaissance*, p. 13.

75 *A Dictionary in Englyshe and Welshe*, 'wrth y darlleawdr'.

76 Quoted in Richard Foster Jones, pp. 13–14.

77 Ibid., p. 173.

78 Ibid., p. 198.

79 Quoted in F. W. Bateson, *English Poetry and the English Language*, p.35.

80 *Shakespeare and Rhetoric*, p. 56.

81 *A treatise of Schemes and Tropes*, 'The Epystle'.

82 Quoted in Richard Foster Jones, p. 92.

83 Ibid., p. 178.

84 Ibid., p. 126.

85 Ibid., p. 76.

86 Ibid., p. 205.

87 Ibid., p. 206.

88 Richard Mulcaster, quoted in Richard Foster Jones, p. 205.

89 *The Arte of English Poesie*, Chapter IX, 'Of Ornament'.

90 Quoted in Albert C. Baugh, p. 285.

91 Quoted in Richard Foster Jones, p. 102.

92 Ibid.

93 Ibid., p. 115.

94 Ibid., p. 117.

95 Ibid., p. 118.

96 Ibid., p. 122.

97 Quoted in Vernon Hall, p. 160.

98 Quoted in Richard Foster Jones, p. 126.

99 Quoted in W. G. Crane, *Wit and Rhetoric in the Renaissance*, pp.122-123.

100 *Shakespeare and Rhetoric*, p. 52.

101 De Witt T. Starnes, *Renaissance Dictionaries*, p. 232.

102 Quoted in De Witt T. Starnes, p. 219.

103 Quoted in Richard Foster Jones, p. 157.

104 Quoted in De Witt T. Starnes, Gertrude E. Noyes, p. 11.

105 'Discourse Concerning Satire' in *Essays of John Dryden*, II, p. 110. Edited by W. P. Ker.

106 Quoted in De Witt T. Starnes, Gertrude E. Noyes, p. 13.

1 Quoted in William Rees, *The Union of England and Wales*, pp. 95–96.

2 As the late Professor W. Ogwen Williams has remarked however, "Since the bulk of the population were monoglot Welsh, the business of the courts could not have been carried on without constant resort to the Welsh language." 'The Survival of the Welsh Language after the Union of England and Wales', *Welsh History Review*, 2, 1, p. 70.

3 David Williams, *A History of Modern Wales*, p. 88. See also Geraint Dyfnallt Owen, *Elizabethan Wales*, p. 204. Dr. Owen rightly points out that "the same treatment was meted out to English in many English schools at that time." See, too, Kenneth Charlton, *Education in Renaissance England*, p. 123.

4 Cardiff MS, 21, p. 469.

5 *Antiquae Linguae Britannicae . . Rudimenta*, 'Praefatio.'

6 cf. D. J. Bowen, 'Gruffudd Hiraethog ac Argyfwng Cerdd Dafod,' *Llên Cymru* II, 3, p. 149, "Yr oedd confensiynau'r canu caeth yn oedrannus iawn erbyn hyn, ond ni chafwyd ymdrech ymhlith y beirdd i ddatblygu dulliau llenyddol newydd."

7 Concern is found in Owen Lewis's letter to Cardinal Guglielmo Sirleto in 1579, edited by Geraint Gruffydd, *Llên Cymru*, II, 1, p. 44:

> "Angli nuper curaruntur suos libros haereticos ex Anglico idiomate conuerti in linguam hanc Britannicam ad inficiendum labe haeretica istas xiij prouincias quae hactenus magis sanae permanserunt quia non intelligerent haereses Anglorum Anglice scriptas. contra hanc fraudem diabolicam ad animas fratrum nostrorum secundum carnem saluandas nos andidotum paramus in istis libris ad illas xiij prouincias transmittendis."

8 *Yny lhyvyr hwnn*, 'Annerch at y darlheawdyr'.

9 *Athravaeth Gristnogavl*, 'Gruphyd fab Rhobert yn annerch . . '.

10 *Eglvryn Phraethineb*, 'Lhythvr Annerch'.

11 *Perl mewn Adfyd*, 'Ir Darllennydd', p. [xx].

12 Quoted in *Rhyddiaith Gymraeg*, *Y gyfrol gyntaf*, p. 138.

13 Leon Battista Alberti. Quoted in Vernon Hall, p. 23.

14 Quoted in *Rhyddiaith Gymraeg*, *Y gyfrol gyntaf*, p. 138.

15 Quoted in De Witt T. Starnes, p. 141.

16 *Dysgeidieth Kristnoges o Verch*, 'Prolog'. Quoted in Garfield H. Hughes, *Rhagymadroddion*, p. viii.

17 Quoted in *The National Library of Wales Journal*, VI, p. 295.

18 *A Dictionary in Englyshe and Welshe*, 'wrth y darlleawdr'.

19 Ibid.

20 From the second address to Rychard Colyngborne at the end of *A briefe and a playne introduction.* Quoted in W. A. Mathias, *Astudiaeth o weithgarwch llenyddol William Salesbury*, p. 415.

21 *Astudiaeth o weithgarwch llenyddol William Salesbury*, pp. 29-30.

22 cf. Arthur Kelton, 'A Commendacion of Welshmen' quoted in *The Bulletin of the Board of Celtic Studies*, XIX, p.249,

"One lawe one loue
One god aboue
And one prencely magestie."

23 *A Dictionary in Englyshe and Welshe*, 'wrth y darlleawdr'.

24 *A Dictionary in Englyshe and Welshe*, 'To the moost victoriouse . . prince Henry . . '. cf. William Morgan, *Y Beibl Cyssegr-lan*, 'Epistola Dedicatoria',

"Quamuis enim eiusdem insulae incolas eiusdem sermonis & loquelae esse magnopere optandum sit: . . "

and Robert Holland, *Basilikon Doron*, 'The Epistle',

"after so long a separation of the Kingdomes of *England* and *Scotland*, and so many diuisions of *Locrinus* and *Cambers* partes, . . beginning in your highnes Ancestors by litle and litle to reconcile and ioyne together what before he had put asunder;"

25 'A copy of the kynges moste gracious Priuilege', found on p. [170] of *Kynniver Llith a Ban*, edited by John Fisher.

26 Quoted in D. R. Thomas, *The life and work of Bishop Davies and William Salesbury*, p. 102.

27 Rowland Vaughan, *Yr Ymarfer o Dduwioldeb*, 1630, 'At y darlleydd'. Quoted in Garfield H. Hughes, p. 119.

28 'The Dialogue of the Government of Wales', printed in *The Description of Penbrokeshire*, Cymmrodorion Record Series, No. 1, Part III (1906), pp. 56–57.

29 pp. 22–23.

30 *Yny lhyvyr hwnn*, 'Annerch at y darlheawdyr'.

31 Ibid.

32 *Oll Synnwyr pen*, 1547, 'wrth y darlleydd'.

33 1587, pp. 51–52. cf. with this, remarks by Sir T. H. Parry-Williams in *Canu Rhydd Cynnar*, p. xxx, concerning books of the seventeenth century,

"Dylid cofio . . fod rhai o hyrwyddwyr y mudiad crefyddol ac addysgol hwn yn credu (ar un adeg, beth bynnag), mai'r peth gorau er iachawdwriaeth y werin fyddai i'r iaith frodorol farw, ac felly arbed poen a thrafferth cyfieithu o iaith estron a chyfansoddi a chyhoeddi ar wahân yn iaith Cymru".

34 *Y Beibl Cyssegr-lan.*

35 *Deffynniad Ffydd Eglwys Loegr*, 'At y Darlleydd', p. (xiv).

36 *Kynniver llith a ban.* Dedicatory letter.

37 Quoted in D. R. Thomas, p. 4.

38 *Athravaeth Gristnogavl*, 'Gruphyd fab Rhobert yn annerch . .'.

39 Quoted in T. H. Parry-Williams, *Canu Rhydd Cynnar*, p. 368.

40 *Perl mewn Adfyd*, 'Ir Darllennydd', p. [xxi].

41 *Antiquae Linguae Britannicae . . Dictionarium Duplex.*

42 Quoted in G. J. Williams, *Traddodiad Llenyddol Morgannwg*, p. 154.

43 Quoted in Richard Foster Jones, p. 33.

44 *Yny lhyvyr hwnn*, "Annerch at y darlheawdyr'.

45 Cardiff MS, 7, p. 555.

46 *Yny lhyvyr hwnn*, 'Annerch at y darlheawdyr'.

47 *Oll Synnwyr pen*, 'wrth y darlleydd'.

48 From the second address to Rychard Colyngborne at the end of *A briefe and a playne introduction*, 1550. Quoted in W. A. Mathias, p. 421.

49 Quoted in D. R. Thomas, p. 101.

50 *Disce Mori Neu Addysg i Farw*, 'Att y Darlleŵydd . .'. Quoted in Garfield H. Hughes, p. 132.

51 *Deffynniad Ffydd Eglwys Loegr*, 'At y Darlleydd', p. [ix].

52 *Perl mewn Adfyd*, 'Ir Darllennydd', p. [xix].

53 Ibid., p. [iv].

54 *The Descripcion of the Sphere or Frame of the Worlde*, 'To his verye louynge Cosen'. Quoted in W. A. Mathias, p. 280.

55 *Oll Synnwyr pen*, 'wrth y darlleydd'.

56 Quoted in *Rhyddiaith Gymraeg*, *Y gyfrol gyntaf*, pp. 10–11.

57 In a letter to Sir William Cecil, quoted in Richard Foster Jones, p. 92.

58 *A Dictionary* . . 'wrth y darlleawdr'.

59 William Salesbury, *Oll Synnwyr pen*, 'wrth y darlleydd'.

60 *Testament newydd ein arglwydd Iesu Christ*, 'Epistol. E.M. at y Cembru'.

61 Ibid.

62 *Gramadeg Cymraeg*, 'Yr Iaith Gymraeg yn erchi . .'.

63 Ibid.

64 *Cambrobrytannicae . . institutiones*, 'At y Cymry'.

65 *Deffynniad Ffydd* . . 'At y Darlleydd' p. [xii].

66 Ibid., 'I'r gwir vrddasol . . ' p. [iii].

67 *Gramadeg Cymraeg*, 'Yr Iaith Gymraeg yn erchi'.

68 *Astudiaeth* . . p. 236.

69 From the second address to Rychard Colyngborne at the end of *A briefe and a playne introduction*, quoted in W. A. Mathias, p. 420.

70 *Cambrobrytannicae . . institutiones*, 'At y Cymry'.

71 Quoted in J. E. Caerwyn Williams, 'Rhyddiaith Grefyddol Cymraeg Canol', *Y Traethodydd* XI, pp. 42–43.

72 Quoted in Richard Foster Jones, p. 73.

73 See R. Geraint Gruffydd, *Religious Prose in Welsh from the Beginning of the Reign of Elizabeth to the Restoration*, 'Conclusion'.

74 *Y Drych Cristianogawl*, 1585, 'at ei garedigion Gymry'. Quoted in Garfield H. Hughes, p. 61.

75 From the second address of William Salesbury to Rychard Colyngborne at the end of *A briefe and a playne introduction*. Quoted in W. A. Mathias, p. 420.

76 Quoted in *Rhyddiaith Gymraeg*, *Y gyfrol gyntaf*, p. 11.

77 *Deffynniad Ffydd* . . 'At y Darlleydd', p. [xiii].

78 *A Dictionary* . . , 'wrth y darlleawdr'.

79 cf. C. H. Conley, *The First English Translators of the Classics*, p. 3,

> "Should it be objected that dedications and prefaces are generally flattering or conventional, the apparently ingenuous, specific, reiterated, and mutually corroborative statements of the translators must be allowed to speak for themselves. . . . It is, . . unlikely that the dedications and prefaces were written without serious purpose".

80 *The Descripcion of the Sphere or Frame of the Worlde*, 'To his verye louynge Cosen . . '. Quoted in W. A. Mathias, p. 280.

81 *Dysgeidieth Kristnoges o Verch*, 'prolog'. Quoted in Garfield H. Hughes, p. viii.

82 (Y Lanter Gristnogawl), 'At y Darllenwr'. Quoted in *Rhyddiaith Gymraeg*, Yr ail gyfrol, pp. 193 and 196.

83 *Theater dv mond*, p. 221.

84 from the second address of William Salesbury to Rychard Colyngborne . . . Quoted in W. A. Mathias, pp. 415–416.

85 Cardiff MS 21, p. 468. For reference that this was a translation of Mosellanus, see W. Alun Mathias, 'Llyfr Rhetoreg William Salesbury', *Llên Cymru* I, 4, p. 263.

86 *A playne and a familiar Introductiō*, 'To my louing Friende Maister Humfrey Toy'. Quoted in W. A. Mathias, p. 423.

87 *Gramadeg Cymraeg*, 'Iaith Gambr yn annerch'.

88 Ibid., 'Y Prylog'.

89 *Y Drych Cristianogawl*, 'at ei garedigion Gymry'. Quoted in Garfield H. Hughes, p. 57.

90 *Deffynniad Ffydd*, 'At y Darlleydd', p. [vii].

91 *Oll Synnwyr pen*, 'wrth y darlleydd'.

92 'at ei garedigion Gymry'. Quoted in Garfield H. Hughes, p. 61.

93 *Y Beibl Cyssegr-lan*, 'Epistola Dedicatoria'.

94 *Gramadeg Cymraeg*. p. [330].

95 Ibid.

96 *Alvearie*, 'Address to the Reader'. Quoted in De Witt T. Starnes, p. 185.

97 'at ei garedigion Gymry'. Quoted in Garfield H. Hughes, p. 53.

98 *Cambrobrytannicae . . institutiones*, 'At y Cymry'.

99 *Oll Synnwyr pen*, 'wrth y darlleydd'.

100 'Rhyddiaith Gymraeg – Rhagarweiniad', *The Transactions of the Honourable Society of Cymmrodorion*, 1948, p. 250.

101 'Lloegr drigiant . .'. Quoted in *Rhyddiaith Gymraeg, Y gyfrol gyntaf*, p.60.

102 *Gramadeg Cymraeg*, 'Yr Iaith Gymraeg yn erchi . . '.

103 Ibid., 'Iaith Gambr yn annerch'.

104 'at ei garedigion Gymry'. Quoted in Garfield H. Hughes, p. 53.

105 *Deffynniad Ffydd*, 'At y Darlleydd', p. [viii].

106 *Gramadeg Cymraeg*, 'Yr Iaith Gymraeg yn erchi . . '.

107 *Cambrobrytannicae . . institutiones*, 'At y Cymry'.

108 Gruffudd Hiraethog, 'Lloegr drigiant . . '. Quoted in D. J. Bowen, '*Gruffudd Hiraethog ac Argyfwng Cerdd Dafod*', Llên Cymru, II, 3, p. 156.

109 cf. D. J. Bowen, ibid., p. 150,

> "Yn y blynyddoedd pan oedd y beirdd yn tuchan o achos diffyg diddordeb yn eu celfyddyd, yr oedd yng Nghymru nifer sylweddol o ddyneiddwyr a eiddigeddai'n fawr wrthynt oherwydd trylwyredd eu gwybodaeth o'r iaith a hanes y genedl".

110 *Oll Synnwyr pen*, 'wrth y darlleydd'.

111 Ibid.

112 Thomas Wiliems, 'Trysawr yr iaith Latin ar Gymraec', quoted in *Rhydd-iaith Gymraeg*, *Y gyfrol gyntaf*, pp. 137–138.

113 Ibid., p. 140.

114 *Testament newydd* . . . 'Epistol. E.M. at y Cembru'.

115 Quoted in Saunders Lewis, 'Damcaniaeth Eglwysig Brotestannaidd', *Efrydiau Catholig* II, p. 43.

116 *Cambrobrytannicae* . . *institutiones*, 'At y Cymry'.

117 *Gramadeg Cymraeg*, 'Iaith Gambr yn annerch'.

1 *A treatise of Schemes and Tropes*, 'The Epystle'.

2 From the second address of William Salesbury to Rychard Colyngborne at the end of *A briefe and a playne introduction*. Quoted in W. A. Mathias, pp. 419–420.

3 *A Treatise Containing the Aequity of an Humble Supplication*, 1587, p. 52.

4 *Cambrobrytannicae . . institutiones*, 'At y Cymry'.

5 *Deffynniad Ffydd*, 'At y Darlleydd', pp. [x – xi].

6 *Gramadeg Cymraeg*, 'Yr Iaith Gymraeg yn erchi . . '.

7 Ibid., pp. [193–194].

8 'at ei garedigion Gymry'. Quoted in Garfield H. Hughes, p. 53.

9 Quoted in Saunders Lewis, 'Damcaniaeth . . ', pp. 51–52.

10 Quoted in Richard Foster Jones, p. 219.

11 See Rosemond Tuve, 'Ancients, Moderns, and Saxons', *Journal of English Literary History*, VI, pp. 165–190,

> "The earliest students of 'Saxon' were churchmen who published works in that language as proof that it was the doctrine now held by Anglicans which had descended unpolluted from earliest times". (p. 165).

See also Stuart Piggott, *Celts, Saxons and the Early Antiquaries*, pp. 12-13.

12 *British Antiquity*, p. 35.

13 *The Blessednes of Brytaine*, or *A Celebration of the Queenes Holyday*, . .

14 *Psalmae Y Brenhinol Brophwyd Dafydd*, 'At y darllenvdd'. Quoted in Garfield H. Hughes, pp. 109–110.

15 *Welsh Reformation Essays*, p. 24.

16 See 'Damcaniaeth . . ', pp. 36–55.

17 *Testament newydd*, Epistol. 'E.M. at y Cembru'.

18 'Damcaniaeth . . ', p. 45. See also Glanmor Williams, *Welsh Reformation Essays*, pp. 194–195.

19 *Testament newydd* . .

20 See Saunders Lewis, 'Damcaniaeth . . ', p. 41.

21 'The Church in Wales in the Age of the Reformation', *Welsh Church Congress, Handbook*, 1953, p. 27.

22 See G. J. Williams, 'Leland a Bale a'r Traddodiad Derwyddol', *Llên Cymru*, IV, 1, p. 17.

23 *Bardhoniaeth, neu brydydhiaeth.*

24 *Eglvryn Phraethineb.*

25 *Antiquae linguae Britannicae rudimenta.* 'Praefatio'.

26 *Kynniver llith a ban.* Dedicatory letter.

27 From the second address to Rychard Colyngborne at the end of *A briefe and a playne introduction.* Quoted in W. A. Mathias, p. 419.

28 David Powel, *The historie of Cambria, containing A description of Cambria .. Sir Iohn Prise .. augmented and made perfect by Humfrey Lhoyd.* p. 4.

29 *The Breuiary of Britayne .. lately Englished by Thomas Twyne,* 1573. Fol. 1

30 Ibid. This list appears at the end of *The Breuiary.*

31 *Psalmae* .. 'At y darllenvdd'. Quoted in Garfield H. Hughes, p. 109.

32 c. 1610. Quoted by John Ballinger in his 'Foreword' to the facsimile edition of *Rhann o Psalmae Dafydd Brophwyd.*

33 David Powel, *The historie .. Humfrey Lhoyd.* p. 4.

34 *Historiae Brytannicae Defensio,* 1573. p. 14.

35 From the second address to Rychard Colyngborne .. 1550. Quoted in W. A. Mathias, p. 416.

36 *Testament newydd,* 'Epistol. E.M. at y Cembru'.

37 Quoted in T. H. Parry-Williams, *Canu Rhydd Cynnar,* p. 368.

38 *A playne and a familiar Introductiō,* 'To my louing Friende Maister Humfrey Toy'. Quoted in W. A. Mathias, pp. 423–424.

39 *Psalmae* .. 'At y darllenvdd'. Quoted in Garfield H. Hughes, p. 109.

40 *Rhann o Psalmae Dafydd Brophwyd,* 1603, 'At y Darlleudd'.

41 'Trysawr yr iaith Latin ar Gymraec', quoted in *Rhyddiaith Gymraeg, Y gyfrol gyntaf,* p. 141.

42 From the Act of Parliament passed in 1563. Quoted by W. Ogwen Williams, 'The Survival of the Welsh Language .. '. *Welsh History Review* 2, 1, p. 70.

43 'The Survival of the Welsh Language .. '. p. 88.

1 Written 1st February, 1582. Quoted by G. J. Williams, *Barddoniaeth neu Brydyddiaeth*, 'Rhagymadrodd', p. 11.

2 'The Church in Wales in the Age of the Reformation', p. 27.

3 Quoted in Richard Foster Jones, p. 79.

4 *Oll Synnwyr pen*, 'wrth y darlleydd'.

5 'Damcaniaeth . . '. p. 50.

6 'at ei garedigion Gymry'. Quoted in Garfield H. Hughes, p. 57.

7 *Cambrobrytannicae . . institutiones*, 'At y Cymry'.

8 *Rhann o Psalmae Dafydd Brophwyd*, 'At y Darlleudd'.

9 'at ei garedigion Gymry'. Quoted in Garfield H. Hughes, p. 53.

10 Quoted in Vernon Hall, *Renaissance Literary Criticism*, p. 35.

11 *Oll Synnwyr pen*, 'wrth y darlleydd'.

12 See *Rhyddiaith Gymraeg*, *Yr ail gyfrol*, p. 21.

13 *Gramadeg Cymraeg gan Gruffydd Robert*, 'Yr Iaith Gymraeg yn erchi . . '

14 'Cowydd Marwnad Wiliam Iarll Penfro', 1570. J. C. Morrice, *Barddoniaeth Wiliam Llŷn*.

15 *Gramadeg Cymraeg*, 'Yr Iaith Gymraeg yn erchi . . '

16 Ibid.

17 'Trysawr yr iaith Latin ar Gymraec', quoted in *Rhyddiaith Gymraeg*, *Y gyfrol gyntaf*, pp. 140–141.

18 Ibid., p. 141.

19 Quoted in G. J. Williams, *Traddodiad Llenyddol Morgannwg*, pp. 195-196

20 'Y Diarebion Camberaec', 1567. Quoted in *Rhyddiaith Gymraeg*, *Y gyfrol gyntaf*, p. 69.

21 *Perl mewn Adfyd*, 'Ir Gwir Barchedic . . ' pp. [vii–viii].

22 Ibid., [vii].

23 *Basilikon Doron*, 'The Epistle'.

24 *Perl mewn Adfyd*, 'Ir Gwir Barchedic . . ' pp. [iv–v].

25 *Deffynniad Ffydd*, 'At y Darlleydd', pp. [viii–ix].

26 *Psalmae* . . , 'At y darllenvdd. Quoted by Garfield H. Hughes, p. 108.

27 *Gramadeg Cymraeg*, 'Iaith Gambr yn annerch'.

28 *Eglvryn Phraethineb*, 'Llythvr Annerch'.

29 *Theater dv mond*, pp. 221–222.

30 Referred to by Mary Augusta Scott, *Elizabethan Translations from the Italian*, p.345.

31 Quoted in W. A. Mathias, p. 48.

32 *Cambrobrytannicae . . institutiones*, 'At y Cymry'.

33 Ibid.

34 *The Triumph of the English Language*, p. 18.

35 See *Rhyddiaith Gymraeg, Y gyfrol gyntaf*, pp. 41, 47, 76.

36 'Trysawr . . '. Quoted in *Rhyddiaith Gymraeg, Y gyfrol gyntaf*, p. 138.

37 Quoted in Clara Gebert, *An Anthology of Elizabethan Dedications and Prefaces*, p. 29.

38 Siôn Dafydd Rhys, *Cambrobrytannicae . . institutiones*, 'At y Cymry'.

39 Ibid.

40 cf. D. R. Thomas, p. 85,

> ". . it brought into common, household use terms that were in existence indeed, but only to be found in scattered MSS: it gave them a definite meaning and a fixity of tenure; it provided a common literary standard".

41 Quoted in *The National Library of Wales Journal*, VI, p. 296.

42 *Cambrobrytannicae . . institutiones*, 'At y Cymry'.

43 *Deffynniad Ffydd*, 'At y Darlleydd', p. [x].

44 *Perl mewn Adfyd*, 'Ir Darllennydd', pp. [xix–xx].

45 *Rhann o Psalmae Dafydd Brophwyd*, 'At y Darlleudd'.

46 Referred to by G. J. Williams, *Gruffydd Robert, Gramadeg Cymraeg* p. xciii.

47 Ibid., p. xcvi

48 *Yny lhyvyr hwnn*, 'Rheol . . '.

49 *A playne and a familiar* . . . Quoted in W. A. Mathias, p. 424.

50 *Deffynniad Ffydd*, At y Darlleydd p. [xii].

51 *Gramadeg Cymraeg gan Gruffydd Robert*, p. xcix, f.n. 5.

52 See Robert A. Hall, *The Italian Questione della Lingua*, p. 16.

53 Siôn Dafydd Rhys, *Cambrobrytannicae . . institutiones*, 'Praefatio'.

54 *Gramadeg Cymraeg*, pp. 8–9.

55 Ibid., title-page.

56 Ibid., p. 8.

57 Ibid., 'Iaith Gambr yn annerch'.

58 'At y Cymry'.

59 Ibid.

60 Siôn Dafydd Rhys, *Cambrobrytannicae . . institutiones*, 'Praefatio'.

61 *Bardhoniaeth, neu brydydhiaeth*, 'Annerch'.

62 'Siôn Dafydd Rhys', *Y Llenor X*, p.40.

63 *The Italian Questione della Lingua*, p. 42.

64 'Praefatio'.

65 *Disce Mori* . . . 'Att y Darlleûydd'. Quoted in Garfield H. Hughes, p. 133.

66 'Damcaniaeth . . ', p. 50.

67 Ibid.

68 Henri Perri, *Eglvryn Phraethineb.* Lhythvr Annerch.

69 Cardiff MS. 21, p. 469.

70 Ibid., p. 468.

71 Ibid.

72 Commendatory verses at the beginning of *Eglvryn Phraethineb.*

73 *Eglvryn Phraethineb*, 'Lhythvr Annerch'.

74 See W. Alun Mathias, 'Llyfr Rhetoreg William Salesbury', *Llên Cymru*, II, 2, pp. 76–77.

75 *Gramadeg Cymraeg*, pp. 69–72.

76 Jesus College MS. 9, pp. 247–292.

77 Cardiff MS. 38, pp. 255–265.

78 *Cambrobrytannicae . . institutiones*, pp. 127–129.

79 British Museum MS. 14,872, pp. 170a–172a.

80 *Antiquae . . rudimenta*, pp. 208–213.

81 cf. Richard Foster Jones, *The Triumph* . . , p. 26, of the position in England,

> "The very strangeness of the earlier dialect, arising from the considerable extent to which the tongue had changed, and also the fact that it was the language of the Middle Ages, a period which did not stand high in the favour of most Englishmen of the sixteenth century, made for depreciation of the earlier language".

82 John Davies, *Antiquae . . rudimenta*, 'Praefatio'.

83 Cardiff MS. 21, p. 469.

84 John Davies, *Antiquae . . rudimenta*, p. 30.

85 See G. J. Williams, *Agweddau ar Hanes Dysg Gymraeg*, pp. 18–19.

86 Ibid., p. 19. Lhuyd died in 1568.

87 Cardiff MS. 21, pp. 467–468.

88 'William Salesbury, Richard Davies and Archbishop Parker', *The National Library of Wales Journal*, II, p. 13.

89 Llanstephan MS. 144. Quoted in G. J. Williams, 'Tri Chof Ynys Brydain', *Llên Cymru*, III, 4, p. 235.

90 For convenience, these collections are referred to by such designations here and elsewhere in this book.

91 *Oll Synnwyr pen*, 'wrth y darlleydd'.

92 Mostyn MS. 204. Quoted in J. G. Evans, *Reports on Manuscripts in the Welsh Language*, Volume I, i, p. 276,

> "Erasmus Botrodamus a scrivenodh lyvr mawr weirthiawg or Direbion lladin ar groeg, . . ".

93 Ibid.

94 *Oll Synnwyr pen*, 'wrth y darlleydd'.

95 cf. Ifor Williams, *Llenyddiaeth Gymraeg Fore*, p. 14,

> "Fel y disgwyliech gan Brotestant newydd eiddgar, awydd ei enaid yw rhoi Beibl i'w genedl. Ond, ysywaeth, nid yw'r iaith Gymraeg arferol yn ddigon llawn i'r pwrpas. Felly ymgais at ei chyfoethogi yw'r llyfr hwn o ddiarhebion, cyforiog o eiriau'r dyddiau gynt, i edrych a fedrir yn nes ymlaen droi Gair Duw iddi".

96 *Oll Synnwyr pen*, 'wrth y darlleydd'.

97 Ibid.

98 Ibid.

99 *Y Diarebion Camberaec.* Quoted in *Rhyddiaith Gymraeg, Y gyfrol gyntaf*, p. 71.

100 Ibid, p. 70.

101 'Ad Lectorem Praefatiuncula'.

102 William Salesbury, *Kynniver llith a ban.* Dedicatory letter.

103 *The Breuiary of Britayne.* Fol. 75b.

104 Quoted in G. J. Williams, *Traddodiad Llenyddol Morgannwg*, p. 210.

105 'at ei garedigion Gymry'. Quoted by Garfield H. Hughes, p. 57.

106 Quoted in Richard Foster Jones, p. 103.

107 Quoted in G. J. Williams, *Gramadeg Cymraeg gan Gruffydd Robert*, p. cxiv.

108 Ibid.

109 Quoted in Vernon Hall, p. 164.

110 cf. D. Gwenallt Jones, *Yr Areithiau Pros*, Rhagymadrodd, p. xix,
"Gellir tybied, yn ôl y *Dewisbethau* a'r *Casbethau*, fod gan yr awduron eu *répertoire* o eiriau cyfansawdd ac ymadroddion, *ornamenta scribendi*. Yr oedd gan brentisiaid, yn ysgolion y beirdd, ystôr ohonynt wrth law i decáu eu Hareithiau".

111 'Praefatio'.

112 *Gramadeg Cymraeg*, pp. [114]–[115].

113 Quoted in *Rhyddiaith Gymraeg, Y gyfrol gyntaf*, p. 11.

114 *Gramadeg Cymraeg*, p. [198].

115 Quoted in G. J. Williams, *Gramadeg Cymraeg gan Gruffydd Robert*, p. cxvii.

116 See Robert A. Hall, *The Italian Questione della Lingua*, p. 46.

117 Quoted in G. J. Williams, *Gramadeg Cymraeg gan Gruffydd Robert*, p. cxvii.

118 *A playne and a familiar Introductiō*, quoted in W. A. Mathias, pp. 60–61.

119 Quoted in W. A. Mathias, pp. 229–230.

120 *Gramadeg Cymraeg*, p. [194].

121 Ibid., pp. [195]–[196].

122 *A Dictionary* . . , 'wrth y darlleawdr'.

123 *Gramadeg Cymraeg*, pp. [203]–[204].

124 Ibid., 'Yr Iaith Gymraeg yn erchi . . '.

125 1562, in an open letter to Sir William Cecil, quoted in Richard Foster Jones, p. 92.

126 *Gramadeg Cymraeg*, pp. [197]–[198].

127 *Opus catechisticum sef yu Sum ne grynodeb* . . p. 585.

128 See Richard Foster Jones, p. 103.

129 *Deffynniad Ffydd*, 'At y Darlleydd', pp. [vi]–[vii].

130 Ibid., p. [vii].

131 Ibid.

132 Ibid., p. [vii]–[viii].

133 *Perl mewn Adfyd*, 'Ir Darllennydd', p. [xxii].

134 *Deffynniad Ffydd*, 'At y Darlleydd', p. [x].

135 Havod MS. 26, p. 204. Quoted in *The Bulletin of the Board of Celtic Studies*, IX, p. 109.

136 'at ei garedigion Gymry', Quoted in Garfield H. Hughes, p. 57.

137 John Hughes. 'Llythyr Annerch'. He explains how he intends to use simple, homely words and expressions. See Geraint Bowen, 'Rhagarweiniad i ryddiaith y gwrth-ddiwygwyr, 1534–1695', *Y Faner*, 29 August, 1951, p. 8.

138 Quoted in Richard Foster Jones, p. 116.

139 *Dysgeidieth Kristnoges o Verch*, 'prolog'. Quoted in Garfield H. Hughes, p. viii.

140 Quoted in Hugh Sykes Davies, 'Sir John Cheke and the Translation of the Bible', *Essays and Studies* (1952), p. 11.

141 'at ei garedigion Gymry'. Quoted in Garfield H. Hughes, p. 57.

142 *Deffynniad Ffydd*, 'At y Darlleydd', p. [vi].

143 *The First Comoedie of Terence, in English . . Carefully translated out of Latin.*

144 *A Treatise of Charitie*. Quoted in Richard Foster Jones, p. 75.

145 *Testament newydd* . . , 'Epistol. E.M. at y Cembru'.

146 *Testament newydd.*

147 Quoted in Richard Foster Jones, p. 113. cf. Henry VIII's comments on the "pestylent gloses in the margentes", see J. Isaacs 'The Sixteenth Century English Versions' in H. Wheeler Robinson, *The Bible in its Ancient and English Versions*, p. 157.

148 Quoted in Albert C. Baugh, *A History of the English Language*, pp. 264–265.

149 *Deffynniad Ffydd*, 'At y Darlleydd', p. [vii].

150 Ibid. Following 'At y Darlleydd'.

151 Quoted in *Rhyddiaith Gymraeg*, *Y gyfrol gyntaf*, p. 138.

152 *A Dictionary* . . 'To the most victoriouse prince Henry'. cf. Cooper's revision of *Bibliotheca Eliotae* 'very nedefull for the knowlage of the latine tonge', quoted by De Witt T. Starnes, p. 69.

153 *Y Drych Cristianogawl*, 'at ei garedigion Gymry'. Quoted in Garfield H. Hughes, p. 57.

154 Quoted in J. G. Evans, *Reports* . . Vol. I, ii, pp. 939–940.

155 Ibid. Vol II, ii, p. 561.

156 Quoted in De Witt T. Starnes, Gertrude E. Noyes, *The English Dictionary from Cawdrey to Johnson*, p. 26.

157 Ibid.

158 Quoted in J. G. Evans, *Reports* . . Vol. I, ii, p. 396.

159 Ibid., p. 358.

160 Ibid., p. 400.

161 Ibid., p. 424.

162 Quoted in J. G. Evans, *Reports* . . Vol. I, iii, p. 1015.

163 Ibid., p. 1059.

164 Quoted in J. G. Evans, *Reports* . . Vol. II, i, p. 336.

165 *A briefe and a playne* . . 'to the Reader'. Quoted by W. A. Mathias, p. 412.

166 cf. remarks by Dennis Jones, *Astudiaeth Feirniadol o Peniarth* 168 *B* (41a–126b), pp. lix–lx,

> "Nid William Salesbury a Gruffydd Robert yn unig a sylweddolodd bwysiced peth ydoedd cyfoethogi geirfa llenorion eu gwlad yn y cyfnod hwn; cawn eirfâu gan Roger Morris a Rhisiart Langford o Drefalun hefyd, ac enwi dau yn unig. Prif amcan y gwŷr hyn a luniodd gasgliadau o eiriau wedi eu tynnu o destunau'r Oesoedd Canol ac o'r iaith fyw ydoedd cyfoethogi geirfa llenorion eu gwlad. . . Y mae'n amlwg, mi gredaf, fod Roger Morris yn astudio'r llawysgrifau Cymraeg a gasglodd, ac nid yn unig yn copïo geirfâu o lyfrau eraill a wnaeth ond llunio rhai ei hun hefyd o'i astudiaethau o'r llawysgrifau er mwyn dwyn y Gymraeg i 'lwybr celfyddyd' fel y mynnai Gruffydd Robert yn ei lyfr".

167 *Gramadeg Cymraeg gan Gruffydd Robert*, p. cxxii.

168 Quoted in J. G. Evans *Reports* . . Vol. I, iii, p. 1015.

169 'Trysawr . . '. Quoted in *Rhyddiaith Gymraeg, Y gyfrol gyntaf*, p. 137.

170 *An English Expositor*, 'To the Courteous Reader'. Quoted by Starnes and Noyes, *The English Dictionary from Cawdrey to Johnson*, p. 20.

171 'Trysawr . . '. Quoted in *Rhyddiaith Gymraeg, Y gyfrol gyntaf*, pp. 137–138.

172 Ibid., p. 141.

173 Ibid., pp. 138–139.

174 Ibid., p. 139.

175 Ibid., p. 138.

176 See J. G. Evans, *Reports* . . Vol. I, ii, xi, for a list of manuscripts in his autograph, also Rhiannon F. Roberts, 'Y Dr. John Davies o Fallwyd', *Llên Cymru* II, 1, pp. 19–35 and II, 2, pp. 97–110.

177 NLW, MS. 14529 E. Quoted by Rhiannon F. Roberts, 'Y Dr. John Davies o Fallwyd' II, *Llên Cymru* II, 2, p. 103.

178 Anthony Wood, *Athenae Oxonienses* II (1815), p. 588.

BIBLIOGRAPHY

Baldwin, C. S., *Renaissance Literary Theory and Practice*, Columbia, 1939.

Barddoniaeth Wiliam Llŷn, ed. J. C. Morrice, Bangor, 1908.

Bateson, F. W., *English Poetry and the English Language*, Oxford, 1934.

Baugh, Albert C., *A History of the English Language*, 2nd ed., New York, 1957.

Bowen, D. J., 'Gruffudd Hiraethog ac Argyfwng Cerdd Dafod', *Llên Cymru*, II, 3, pp. 147–160, Cardiff, 1953.
Gruffudd Hiraethog a'i Oes, Cardiff, 1958.

Bowen, Geraint, 'Rhagarweiniad i ryddiaith y gwrth-ddiwygwyr, 1534–1695', *Y Faner*, 29 August, 1951.

Charlton, Kenneth, *Education in Renaissance England*, London, 1965.

Clark, D. L., *Rhetoric and Poetry in the Renaissance*, Columbia, 1922.

Clynnog, Morys, *Athravaeth Gristnogavl*, with an introduction by Gruffydd Robert, Milan, 1568. Reprint issued by the Honourable Society of Cymmrodorion, London, 1880.

Conley, C. H., *The First English Translators of the Classics*, Yale, 1927.

Crane, W. G., *Wit and Rhetoric in the Renaissance*, Columbia, 1937.

Davies, Hugh Sykes, 'Sir John Cheke and the Translation of the Bible', *Essays and Studies*, 1952.

Davies, John, *Antiquae linguae Britannicae rudimenta*, London, 1621.
Antiquae linguae Britannicae et linguae Latinae, dictionarium duplex, London, 1632.

The Dictionary of Welsh Biography, under the auspices of the Honourable Society of Cymmrodorion, Blackwell, 1959.

Dodd, A. H., 'The Church in Wales in the Age of the Reformation', *Welsh Church Congress Handbook*, 1953.

Y Drych Cristianogawl, Rouen, 1585.

Ewert, Alfred, *The French Language*, London, 1938.

Flower, Robin, 'William Salesbury, Richard Davies, and Archbishop Parker', *The National Library of Wales Journal*, II, i, Aberystwyth, 1941.

Gebert, Clara, *An Anthology of Elizabethan Dedications and Prefaces*, Pennsylvania, 1933.

Gruffydd, R. Geraint, 'Dau Lythyr gan Owen Lewis', *Llên Cymru*, II, 1,36-45, Cardiff, 1952.
Religious Prose in Welsh from the beginning of the reign of Elizabeth to the Restoration. University of Oxford D.Phil thesis, 1952.

Hall, Robert A., *The Italian Questione della Lingua*, Chapel Hill, 1942.

Hall (Jr.), Vernon, *Renaissance Literary Criticism*, Columbia, 1945.

Holland, Robert, *Basilikon Doron: Nev, Athrawiaeth i Fawredh*, London, 1604. Reproduced in facsimile with a bibliographical note by John Ballinger, Cardiff, 1931.

Hughes, Garfield, H., *Rhagymadroddion 1547–1659*, Cardiff, 1951.

Isaacs, J., 'The Sixteenth-Century English Versions' in *The Bible in its Ancient and English Versions*, ed. H. Wheeler Robinson, Oxford, 1940.

Jones, D. Gwenallt, *Yr Areithiau Pros*, Cardiff, 1934.

Jones, Dennis, *Astudiaeth feirniadol o Peniarth 168 B (41a–126b)*. University of Wales M.A. thesis, 1954.

Jones, Richard Foster, *The Triumph of the English Language*, Stanford, 1951.

Jones, Thomas, 'Pre-Reformation Welsh Versions of the Scriptures', *The National Library of Wales Journal*, IV, Aberystwyth, 1945.

Kendrick, T. D., *British Antiquity*, London, 1950.

Kyffin, Edward, *Rhann o Psalmae Dafydd Brophwyd*, London, 1603. Facsimile edition with Foreword by John Ballinger, Cardiff, 1930.

Kyffin, Morris, *Andria. The first Comoedie of Terence, in English . . Carefully translated out of Latin*, London, 1588.
The Blessednes of Brytaine, or A Celebration of the Queenes Holyday, London, 1587.
Deffynniad Ffydd Eglvvys Loegr, 1595. Reprint edited by Wm. Prichard Williams, Bangor, 1908.

Lewis, C. S., *English Literature in the Sixteenth Century Excluding Drama*, Oxford, 1954.

Lewys, Huw, *Perl mewn Adfyd*, Oxford, 1595. Reprint edited by W. J. Gruffydd, Cardiff, 1929.

Lewis, Saunders, 'Damcaniaeth Eglwysig Brotestannaidd', *Efrydiau Catholig* II, Aberystwyth, 1947.

Lhuyd, Humphrey, *The Breuiary of Britayne lately Englished by Thomas Twyne*, London, 1573.

Mathias, W. Alun, *Astudiaeth o weithgarwch llenyddol William Salesbury*. University of Wales M.A. Thesis, 1949.
'Llyfr Rhetoreg William Salesbury', *Llên Cymru* I, 4, pp. 259–268, Cardiff, 1951, and *Llên Cymru* II, 2, pp. 71–81, Cardiff, 1952.

Midleton, Wiliam, *Bardhoniaeth, neu brydydhiaeth*, . . London, 1593. Reprint edited by G. J. Williams, Cardiff, 1930.

Moore, J. L., *Tudor-Stuart Views on the Growth Status and Destiny of the English Language*, Halle, 1910.

Morgan, T. J., 'Rhyddiaith Gymraeg, Rhagarweiniad', *The Transactions of the Honourable Society of Cymmrodorion*, London, 1948.

Morgan, William, *Y Beibl cyssegr-lan*, London, 1588.

Owen, George, 'The Dialogue of the Government of Wales', printed in *The Description of Penbrokeshire*, Cymmrodorion Record Series No. I, Part III, London, 1906.

Owen, Geraint Dyfnallt, *Elizabethan Wales*, Cardiff, 1962.

Parry, T., 'Siôn Dafydd Rhys', *Y Llenor*, X, pp. 35–45, Wrexham, 1931.
A History of Welsh Literature, trans. Idris Bell, Oxford, 1955.

Parry-Williams, T. H. (Editor), *Canu Rhydd Cynnar*, Cardiff, 1932.

Penry, John, *A Treatise Containing the Aequity of an Humble Supplication*, Oxford, 1587.

Perri, Henri, *Eglvryn Phraethineb*, London, 1595. Facsimile edition by G. J. Williams, Cardiff, 1930.

Piggott, Stuart, *Celts, Saxons, and the Early Antiquaries*, Edinburgh, 1967.

Pollard, A. W., and Redgrave, G. R., *A Short-Title Catalogue of Books Printed in England, Scotland, and Ireland and of English Books printed abroad, 1475–1640*, London, 1926.

Powel, David, *The historie of Cambria, containing A description of Cambria . . augmented and made perfect by Humfrey Lhoyd*, London, 1584.

Prys, John, *Yny lhyvyr hwnn*, London, 1547. Reprint edited by John H. Davies, Bangor, 1902.
Historiae Brytannicae Defensio, London, 1573.

Puttenham, George, *The Arte of English Poesie*, ed. Gladys Doidge Willcock, Alice Walker, Cambridge, 1936.

Rees, William, 'The Union of England and Wales', *Transactions of the Honourable Society of Cymmrodorion*, London, 1937.

Reports on Manuscripts in the Welsh Language, J. Gwenogvryn Evans, London, 1898–1910.

Rhyddiaith Gymraeg: Y gyfrol gyntaf, 'Detholion o Lawysgrifau, 1488–1609', ed. T. H. Parry-Williams, Cardiff, 1954.

Rhyddiaith Gymraeg: Yr ail gyfrol, 'Detholion o Lawysgrifau a Llyfrau Printiedig, 1547-1618' ed. Thomas Jones, Cardiff, 1956.

Rhys, John David (Siôn Dafydd), *Cambrobrytannicae cymraecaeue linguae institutiones*, London, 1592.

Robert, Gruffydd, *Gramadeg Cymraeg*, ed. G. J. Williams, Cardiff, 1939.

Roberts, Rhiannon, F., 'Y Dr. John Davies o Fallwyd', *Llên Cymru*, II, 1, pp. 19–35 and *Llên* Cymru II, 2, pp. 97–110, Cardiff, 1952.

Rubel, Veré L., *Poetic Diction in the English Renaissance*, New York, 1941.

Salesbury, William, *Oll Synnwyr pen*, London, 1547. Reprint edited by J. Gwenogvryn Evans, Bangor, 1902.
A dictionary in Englyshe and Welshe, London, 1547. Reprinted in four parts for the Honourable Society of Cymmrodorion, London, 1877.
Kynniver llith a ban, London, 1551. Reprint edited by John Fisher, Cardiff, 1931.

Scott, Mary Augusta, *Elizabethan Translations from the Italian*, Boston, 1916.

Sherry, Richard, *A treatise of schemes & tropes*, London, 1550.

Simon, Joan, *Education and Society in Tudor England*, Cambridge, 1966.

{ Smyth, D. R., *Crynnodeb o Adysc Cristnogaul*, Paris, 1609.
Smyth, Rhosier, *Theater dv mond sef ivv Gorsedd y byd*. Paris, 1615. Reprint edited by T. Parry, Cardiff, 1930.

Starnes, De Witt T., *Renaissance Dictionaries*, Texas, 1954.

Starnes, De Witt T., and Noyes, Gertrude, E. *The English Dictionary from Cawdrey to Johnson 1604–1755*, N. Carolina, 1946.

Testament newydd ein arglwydd Iesu Christ, London, 1567.

Thomas, D. R., *The life and work of Bishop Davies and William Salesbury*, Oswestry, 1902.

Tuve, Rosemond, 'Ancients, Moderns, and Saxons', *Journal of English Literary History*, VI, Baltimore, 1939.

Weinberg, Bernard, *Critical Prefaces of the French Renaissance*, Illinois, 1950.

Welsh in Education and Life, H.M.S.O., London, 1927.

Willcock, Gladys D., 'Shakespeare and Rhetoric', *Essays and Studies*, 1943.

Williams, David, *A History of Modern Wales*, London, 1950.

Williams, Glanmor, *Bywyd ac Amserau'r Esgob Richard Davies*, Cardiff, 1953.
The Welsh Church from Conquest to Reformation, Cardiff, 1962.
Dadeni, Diwygiad a Diwylliant Cymru, Cardiff, 1964.
Welsh Reformation Essays, Cardiff, 1967.

Williams, G. J., *Traddodiad Llenyddol Morgannwg*, Cardiff, 1948.
'Tri Chof Ynys Brydain', *Llên Cymru*, III, 4, pp. 234–239, Cardiff, 1955.
'Leland a Bale a'r Traddodiad Derwyddol', *Llên Cymru*, IV, 1, pp. 15–25, Cardiff, 1956.
Agweddau ar Hanes Dysg Gymraeg, edited by Aneirin Lewis, Cardiff, 1969.

Williams, I. M., *Hanesyddiaeth yng Nghymru yn yr unfed ganrif ar bymtheg gan gyfeirio'n arbennig at Humphrey Lhuyd a David Powel*. University of Wales M.A. thesis, 1951.
'Ysgolheictod Hanesyddol yr Unfed Ganrif ar Bymtheg', *Llên Cymru*, II, 2, pp. 111–124, Cardiff, 1952, and *Llên Cymru*, II, 4, pp. 209–223, Cardiff, 1953.

Williams, Ifor, *Llenyddiaeth Gymraeg Fore*, Traethodau'r Deyrnas, Wrexham, 1924.

Williams, J. E. Caerwyn, 'Rhyddiaith Grefyddol Cymraeg Canol', *Y Traethodydd*, XI, pp. 36–43, 1942.

Williams, W. Ogwen, *Tudor Gwynedd*, Caernarvon, 1958.
'The Survival of the Welsh Language after the Union of England and Wales: the first phase, 1536–1642', *Welsh History Review*, Vol. 2, No. 1, Cardiff, 1964.

Wood, Anthony à, *Athenae Oxonienses*, London, 1815.

Wright, Louis B., *Middle-Class Culture in Elizabethan England*, N. Carolina, 1935.